Evergreen Beach Hotel

❖ COOKBOOK ❖

100 Years of Family Hospitality

DOOR COUNTY, WISCONSIN

Enjoy hotel memories and wonderful family recipes

Joyce Gerdman 2004

by Joyce Knudson Gerdman

First Edition

Published by
Joyce Knudson Gerdman Publishing
PO Box 170
Ephraim, Wisconsin 54211

ISBN: 0-942495-82-9

Library of Congress Number: 98-066483

Printed in the United States of America by
Palmer Publications, Inc.
318 N. Main Street
Amherst, WI 54406

Designed by
Amherst Press
A division of Palmer Publications, Inc.

Dedication

With love and warm memories,

I dedicate this book to my Mother and Dad

who inspired us to be the best that we could be.

Floyd and Laurel Knudson

Contents

Evergreen Beach Gazebo

Across green esplanades
the lake breeze
stirs the murmurs
of summer memories
caught in a spider's wheel
the white vaulted roof beams
of this empty gazebo
Nervous giggles, first kisses
long goodbyes at summer's end
Rustle of lace and satin
trembling voices
wedding vows
Guitar chords
voices in harmony
ice cream churn
steady rhythm
Soft lullaby chanting
mother rocking her toddler to sleep
Faint crack of ice
spoons clink in tall glasses
lemonade and sweet tea
Listen
waves on the lakeshore
grandmother's hands
turning the pages
in her family album

—Lauren Mittermann

Acknowledgments

This cookbook was something I thought about doing for many years, when one day last fall, Evelyn Haase, who has been coming to the hotel for years, said to me, "Did you do a centennial cookbook?" Then she said, "You should really do one." So I decided then and there to get started and I thank Evelyn for her encouragement.

A special thank you to my husband Glenn, who was such a help getting everything on computer disks and for taking some outstanding photographs throughout the years.

Thanks to my daughters Diane Jacobson and Shelley Cox for supporting me and helping me locate old hotel recipes and pictures. I'm thankful for my grandchildren, Britta, Elaine, Karin, Laurel and Steven who bring so much joy into my life.

Thank you to Lauren Mittermann for her beautiful poem "Evergreen Beach Gazebo", a teacher and storyteller as well as a poet.

Thank you to Elaine Zarse who waitressed with me in those early days and shared her Grandmother Annie Olson's homemade ice cream recipe. We both loved that ice cream.

Thank you to Walter and Mary Hirthe for the picture of Fordel Hogenson and information on the schooner *Ebenezer*.

Thank you to my sisters Grace Vernon and Evelyn Albrecht, and to nieces Janel, Annette, Terri and Melissa for sharing favorite family recipes with me.

Thanks to artist Charles Peterson for letting us use his india ink drawing of the *Ebenezer*, which Fordel Hogenson called "Loading Lumber in Ephraim."

A special thanks to Amherst Press for all their help and for believing we could have the cookbook ready by June, 1998.

Lastly, thanks to all the hotel staff, past and present, who always carried on the tradition of hospitality, which makes Evergreen Beach a very special place.

Introduction

Having worked in various hotels in Ephraim, before becoming innkeepers, didn't prepare Floyd and Laurel Knudson for the challenge of owning and operating a hotel. My dad, Floyd, was willing to tackle all the improvement projects, and my mother, Laurel, didn't mind doing the office work, but serving three meals a day, even though each enjoyed cooking, turned out to be a learning experience. My mother had a large collection of recipes which helped them get started. Relatives had cooked on ships, in restaurants and hotels, and gave them helpful advice. I think the reason they became so successful was because they both worked long and hard as a team.

Before we arrived as owners, my parents had a well organized hotel and kitchen, and since we had spent every summer since 1955, helping, it was easier for us. After Glenn graduated from the University of Wisconsin, Oshkosh, he taught sixth grade, for ten years, at Tess Corners, near Waukesha, where we lived. Our daughters, Diane and Shelley, attended school in Waukesha. In 1969, Glenn was offered a contract to teach seventh and eighth grade math in a new junior high, just what he wanted.

That same year, my parents decided they wanted to retire. Since we loved Ephraim, had a house there, had helped every summer vacation at the hotel, we felt we should buy the hotel when the school year ended. Glenn was able to get a teaching position in Gibraltar Schools, and eventually he became the junior high math teacher. The school year overlapped the "season", but we were able to work it out so everything got done.

From 1969 to 1976, we served breakfast between 7:00 and 10 a.m. I remember getting up at 5 a.m. to bake coffee cake, get bacon, eggs, coffee, pancake batter and grill ready to go at 7 a.m. When we remodeled into new motel rooms in 1976, it was a wonderful relief not to get up so early to make breakfast. Since then, we serve hot coffee and fresh rolls when the office opens at 8 a.m.

In 1979, our daughter Diane married Larry Jacobson on April 28 and just six weeks later Shelley married John Cox on June 8, Shelley's grandparents 50th wedding anniversary. That was a busy spring, having two weddings, our Brazilian exchange student, Gláucia Delgado, living with us and getting the hotel cleaned and ready for the summer.

Both daughters graduated from college, Diane from the University of Wisconsin, Eau Claire in December 1978, in elementary education and Shelley from the University of Wisconsin, Stevens Point in December 1979, in early childhood education. Shelley is a kindergarten teacher at Gibraltar. After doing substitute teaching at Gibraltar, Diane became the bookkeeper for

Larry's Amoco business. I taught in an elementary school for two years after graduating from Door-Kewaunee Teachers College, so our whole family were teachers.

Both daughters have been a great help in the hotel operations, working in the office or choosing new furnishings, with John keeping the lawn, beach and buildings in good shape and Larry lending a hand with painting and repairs when needed. They all work in many aspects of the business and are an inspiration to us. As they get older, the grandchildren help with cleaning rooms, sweeping decks, wiping off lawn chairs, pulling weeds in the flowers and beach and watering flower pots and baskets. I'm filled with love and pride in them.

In it's 100 years of operation, the hotel has been run by only two families, the Hogensons and the Knudson/Gerdmans. We feel that maintaining the same high standards through the years will continue with Diane and Shelley and their families. May your enjoyment be complete with these wonderful recipes and memories from the Evergreen Beach Hotel.

History of the Evergreen Beach Hotel

The Evergreen Beach Hotel has been a part of historical Ephraim for over one hundred years. By 1896, a large number of tourists were coming to Ephraim, in Door County, Wisconsin, and Captain Fordel Hogenson could see a need for more accommodations. He began by taking visitors into his home, but soon found the need to add on to his house to accommodate the growing number of guests.

   Along with his parents, Fordel Hogenson emigrated from Norway, and settled in Ephraim in 1873. He worked as a carpenter, a trade he learned in Norway. In 1875, he married Lena Reinartsen and they became the parents of seven children. Lena died in 1887; he married Tonette Tonneson the next year. Around this time, he decided he would build a sailing schooner to transport cargo for northern Door County.

Fordel Hogenson

On the beach in front of the present hotel, Fordel and his sons constructed the three-masted schooner. He called it the *Ebenezer*. It was launched from the beach, and was the only schooner built in Ephraim. Parts of the *Ebenezer* lie buried in the sand across from the Evergreen Beach Hotel, to this day. It had run aground in front of the hotel and was left to rot and decay. Old-timers mention seeing the skeleton of the schooner while walking by the hotel on their way to school as children.

Just before he began building the hotel, in 1896, Fordel worked as a carpenter on the complete remodeling of the Moravian Church in Ephraim. He was an active member of the church and community.

In 1896, he sailed the *Ebenezer* to Menominee, Michigan, and brought back enough lumber to build the hotel, which was added on to his homestead.

When the hotel was finished, it consisted of three floors, with a porch that surrounded the entire building. In the morning the guests would sit in the sun on the east side, then move to the west side in the afternoon, facing the harbor.

The first floor included a kitchen, dining room, office, lobby with fireplace, and the family living quarters. The second and third floors were made up of twenty-two bedrooms including bedrooms from the original house. Some of the bedrooms were small, with one

single bed. Each room was furnished with a wooden bed with a fancy high headboard, dresser, and washstand on which was placed a washbowl, pitcher and matching soap dish. Meals were twenty-five cents per person. Room and board was five dollars a week per person. Three meals a day, served family style, was called the American Plan.

After Fordel Hogenson died in 1927, his wife Tonette married Edward Evenson. Tonette called on family friend Peder Knudson, to run the hotel for her, the summer after Peder's wife died. Peder had been the chef on the Great Lakes passenger ship *Bon Ami* of the Goodrich Steamer Line and had settled in Door County. She said, "It was a Godsend that Peder came," because he made money for them. Later, Peder married Fordel's daughter, Dena Hogenson. Peder's nephew was Floyd Knudson (my father).

Fordel's son Herman and his wife Lily took over the management of the hotel in 1928. They operated the hotel for about sixteen years. In the early thirties, a large bathroom with tub was added on the second floor. Two bathrooms, one for men and one for women, were added to the third floor. Herman charged twenty-five cents for the use of the tub, with hot water, which had to be heated on the kitchen stove. The hotel guests were summoned to meals by the ringing of a large dinner bell.

Many guests arrived by steamer at the Anderson dock, where they were met by horse and buggy to be escorted to the hotel. Some guests came by train to the Green Bay and Western station, in Sturgeon Bay. There they would be met by Frank Anderson and his cab, which brought them to Ephraim. Many guests, in the early days, stayed for the summer.

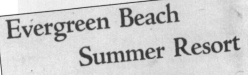

Evergreen Beach Summer Resort

is situated in the Village of Ephraim, Wis. It is surrounded with a beautiful woods of Evergreens, except on the West that faces the waters of Eagle Bay, and has the nicest kind of Bathing Beach.

It is especially noted for it Tested Pure Spring Water and Home Cooking.

Accommodates about fifty guests

H. D. HOGENSON, Prop.

Ephraim, Wisconsin

Some of the activities available for tourists in those early days were swimming, boating, hiking, horseback riding, fishing, picnicking, and the Sunday night sings at the village hall. Walking to Wilson's Ice Cream Parlor for ice cream and other treats was a favorite pastime, and to this day it still is popular with the guests.

In the winter, the harbor ice was cut into square blocks and stored in sawdust in the icehouse. Covering the ice with sawdust insulated it from the warm air, and ice would be available all summer. This practice was continued well into the 1940s. I can remember my father, Floyd, putting up ice in the hotel icehouse to use in the summertime.

It was in 1944 that Floyd and Laurel Knudson (my mother)

began operating the hotel, having purchased it from the Hogenson
estate. Floyd had come to know the hotel through his uncle, Peder
Knudson. It is interesting that both Floyd and Laurel Johnson
Knudson's parents had emigrated to Door County from Norway,
as the Hogensons had.

Immediately, Floyd began to put a lot of work into the hotel
to modernize it for the times. Laurel was a trained bookkeeper
and she became the manager. Their four daughters—myself
(Joyce), Grace, Evelyn, and Elaine—helped out with waitressing,
folding laundry and cleaning. In those early days the family did
nearly everything themselves, with the help of a small staff. Floyd
divided smaller rooms on the second floor to make a bath for
each room. He put new electric wiring in all the rooms and
sanded and varnished all the hardwood floors on the first floor.
He did all this while still working in the shipyard in Sturgeon Bay.
Laurel had a friend who hung new wallpaper in the dining room
and lobby. Rose Bradley, another friend, gave her wall hangings
and pictures from her trips around the world, to decorate the dining room and office. All the bedrooms were given a fresh coat of

paint and furnished with new bedspreads or quilts, and curtains.

After ending his shipyard job, Floyd also worked at landscaping the front yard by moving part of the hill behind the hotel by hand to the front of the hotel. To keep the rest of the hill from sliding down, he built a retaining wall from the stone taken from the hill, four feet high and about sixty feet long, that still stands today. He began the tradition of planting petunias down the front walk. At first they were a combination of colors, but he found the pink petunias were able to hold up better in rain and heat, so now they have become a trademark for the hotel.

Becoming innkeepers included serving three meals a day, which continued until 1956 (then only breakfast until 1976). Each hotel had a different dinner bell that they rang when mealtime was near. While my sisters and I waitressed, Floyd helped with the cooking. I remember he would flip the pancakes for breakfast and when he finished an order, he hurried out back to turn the ice cream churn by hand, so we could have homemade ice cream for Sunday noon chicken dinner. Laurel would make up the daily menus every week. Usually we served one entree for dinner each night, with a choice of soup or juice and a choice of dessert. Guests would sit at the same table for all their meals and have the same waitress for their stay. The guests usually stayed a week or more.

During this time, as in earlier days, all the laundry was done by hand at the hotel, usually by extra cleaning help or family, and without the convenience of dryers. We used a wringer-washer with two tubs of water. This was done in a separate building.

Laurel made several trips with the Chamber of Commerce to Chicago to promote Door County at the Tourism Trade Show, where they would hand out brochures about Door County. One summer Floyd and Laurel arranged with a travel agency to bring people from Chicago for weekends. They would come by train to Manitowoc where they were met by the Lake and Bayview Bus lines which brought them to the hotel around 11:00 p.m. on Friday night. Floyd and Ollie Allyn, who were helping us at the hotel, would sit out on the front porch and wait

for the bus. Sometimes it would be late and sometimes there would be extra people. One time there were two extra women. My dad introduced them to two women who had a room with two double beds, and then asked if they could all share a room until the next day when he could find another room. The one woman had her arms crossed and, standing firm, said, "I won't share a room with total strangers." Dad called Adolph Anderson and found a room for them in their private home at midnight. Arrangements were made with South Shore Pier to take these guests on a cruise around Eagle Harbor. When it rained they took the guests, with many cars, for a tour through Peninsula State Park. Rain or shine, the guests had a good time.

When visitors began requesting more private accommodations, Floyd added double cottages on the lawn and on the beach. One of the regular guests wished she had a fireplace in her favorite cottage, so that fall, Floyd added a fireplace in that cottage. Needless to say, this guest was very excited when she came back the following year and saw the fireplace.

While the younger daughters, Evelyn and Elaine, waitressed, Grace operated the Western Union terminal in a room next to the hotel office in the mid-1950s. She was the sole operator each summer. She received telegrams from the Sturgeon Bay office, and hand-delivered those for the Ephraim area, while phoning in those for outside Ephraim. Grace's son, Floyd Edward, was born in 1956 on his grandfather's birthday. He would sit in his buggy beside her and smile at all of the Western Union customers.

Starting in 1955, Floyd and Laurel began spending several months in Winter Haven, Florida. They purchased a home there, and would leave the end of October, and return to Ephraim in April. Floyd enjoyed gardening, so could pursue that hobby all year. Their Florida backyard was full of orange and grapefruit trees as well as flowers.

Guests were served three meals a day up until 1956. After that we served breakfast only, included with your room. Guests enjoyed those special breakfasts, with fresh fruit, juice, cereal, eggs with bacon or sausage, French toast or buttermilk pancakes served with hot coffee and a basket of fresh coffee cake. Breakfast was served between seven and ten every day.

On July 29, 1959, the day began as usual, with the hotel full of guests. I was busy in the hotel kitchen preparing breakfast, while my youngest sister, Elaine, was serving the guests in the dining room. It was a hot summer day and we were anxious to finish breakfast and our cleaning chores so we could go swimming. Around noon, Elaine and a friend left for Fish Creek. They were in a head-on collision with another car between Fish Creek and Ephraim. Both girls were injured, Elaine's friend less severely. We all rushed to the hospital to be with Elaine. At first we prayed that she would live, but hearing how seriously she was hurt, we prayed for what was best for her. She died July 30, 1959. She was a dearly beloved sister and touched so many lives in her short eighteen years. Our family, friends, and our Moravian Church, helped us through this difficult time. Both Floyd and Laurel were lifetime members of the Moravian Church which gave them strength to deal with such a great loss. This was a life-changing experience for all of us.

As the years went by, we did need to hire more people. We had three or four college students for waitressing, a young man to mow lawn and do dishes, and usually three cooks besides the family. The waitresses helped clean the rooms after breakfast. We also began sending our laundry out which gave us more time with the guests. During this time, guests usually stayed a week or more, but some guests, like Gaylord Wilkenson, (an artist), Helen Walton from Rockford, and Mr. and Mrs. Teuber from Chicago, spent the whole summer. Most guests came by car at this time, but a few took the train to Manitowoc and then the bus which brought them to Ephraim. It wasn't long before people began coming up for just long weekends.

For ten years, up until 1965, smorgasbord was served on Tuesday and Saturday nights, by reservation. This was open to the public and grew to be very popular. We had half of our kitchen partitioned off, so the guests could circle around two long buffet tables. Floyd prepared the Norwegian meatballs, baked chicken, roast pork or turkey, and liver paté. Laurel made small open-faced sandwiches and many different salads, including our famous tuna salad fish mold. The cooks made Swedish tea rings, rolls, lefse, potatoes, baked beans, and bowls of herring, pickled beets, pickled apples, other salads, and platters of cheese. My husband, Glenn, carved a watermelon basket, complete with handle, and filled it with fresh fruit. I baked cherry pies for dessert, while Mrs. Norman made her famous hot fudge sauce. It was definitely a meal to remember. We spent days getting everything ready, preparing food, mopping the hardwood dining and kitchen floors. I was in charge of putting bowls of fresh flowers on all the tables. Everyone took great pride in making each smorgasbord special.

The recreational activities grew to include golf, tennis, increased boating, charter fishing, wind surfing, the Peninsula Music Festival (started by conductor Thor Johnson), the Peninsula Players theater, the outdoor American Folklore theater, Birch Creek Music Center, art galleries and many different kinds of shops. The Door Community Auditorium is open year-round, with exciting performances by world-renowned artists.

In 1969 Glenn and I bought the hotel from my parents. Glenn was teaching at Gibraltar Area Schools and the season barely overlapped the school year. We began modernizing to accommodate the changing tastes of the visitors. We continued to serve a full breakfast; Aunt Irene Knudson and I were the chief cooks.

The traditional Scandinavian Fyr-Bal ceremony in June recognizes an Ephraim resident each year who has given graciously to the community. Floyd Knudson was honored as chieftain in 1973, then twenty years later, in 1993, I had the honor bestowed on me. The ceremony ends with the lighting of bonfires along the shore to burn the winter witch, which means the end of winter and the beginning of summer.

The hotel was completely renovated in 1976 into two floors of large, comfortable motel accommodations. The work went on all winter and spring, with Glenn and me sweeping up every night, the lathes and plaster that the carpenters tore apart during the day. When finished, the new rooms, with covered decks, were all overlooking Eagle Harbor and the most spectacular sunsets imaginable. We discontinued serving breakfast, but still serve hot coffee, tea and fresh rolls each morning.

Six years later, we added a second floor with four new rooms to the South Lodge and removed the remaining cottages. Four deluxe rooms with king-sized beds were added to the north end of the hotel in 1988. Our four beachside rooms, located on the water, were remodeled with covered decks.

We restored all the antique dressers and use them, along with handmade oak armoires, for the television sets as well as cabinets for the refrigerators and microwaves. There are double, queen or king-sized beds, air-conditioning, full baths and telephones.

There has always been a sand beach in front of Evergreen Beach but a heated outdoor pool was added to the front lawn in

1983 for swimming and relaxing. Floyd had built a dock with cribs and boards. When it began to break up from the ice and storms, we had John Fitzgerald build a dock with steel sides and a concrete top. He saved the little house Floyd had built on the end of his dock and placed it back on the new dock, where it's still used today.

The refurbishing of the original hotel and newer buildings is an ongoing process, in which the comfort of the guests is always put first. We're proud of all the improvements we've made, from furnishings to flowers to landscaping, while preserving the charm of the original.

One of the things you will still find at the Evergreen Beach is the family atmosphere. Our children, Diane and Larry Jacobson

and Shelley and John Cox, help us run the hotel operations. Along with our five grandchildren on the premises helping out, it makes four generations of my family who have worked at the Evergreen Beach Hotel.

Our summer of 1997 was a celebration of the 100th year anniversary of the Evergreen Beach Hotel. Our centennial events included a birthday cake, an ice cream sundae party, and two catered picnics, one in July and one in August, with our cousins from Norway, our exchange student, Bebel Delgado (Gláucia's sister) from Brazil, a friend from Paris, plus friends and family from all over the country. It was a very nostalgic time for our family.

When Floyd and Laurel owned the hotel, it was open from Memorial Day to Labor Day, but in recent years autumns have become a favorite time to vacation, to view the fall colors, or attend a fall festival. Visitors flock to Door County each May

for the Festival of Blossoms. Over 1 million daffodils, along with wildflowers and our famous cherry and apple blossoms are the main attraction for this festival. To accommodate all of our guests, the resort is now open from early May until the end of October.

Our family looks forward to each new season. The tradition of hospitality, which began one hundred years ago, continues with our daughters and their families. Being innkeepers has always been interesting and exciting and we can't imagine doing anything else. We've met so many wonderful people who have enriched our lives. Our family looks forward to a future of serving Door County visitors.

Joyce Knudson Gerdman

Breakfast

Bran Muffins

yield: 12 muffins

1	cup whole-bran cereal
1	cup flour
1/4	cup sugar
1	tablespoon baking powder
1/2	teaspoon salt
1	egg
1	cup milk
1/4	cup vegetable oil

Preheat oven to 400 degrees. Grease 12-cup muffin tin.

In medium bowl using a fork, mix bran cereal, flour, sugar, baking powder, and salt. In a small bowl using a fork, beat egg slightly; stir in milk and oil.

Add egg mixture to flour mixture. Using a spoon, stir just until flour is moistened. Spoon batter into baking cups.

Bake 25 minutes. Immediately remove muffins from pan to cool.

Oatmeal Raisin Muffins

yield: 12 muffins

1 cup flour
1 tablespoon baking powder
1/2 teaspoon salt
1/4 cup shortening
1 cup rolled oats
1 egg
1 cup milk
1/2 cup brown sugar
1/2 cup raisins
1/4 cup sugar
1/4 teaspoon cinnamon

Preheat oven to 425 degrees. Line 12-cup muffin tin with paper baking cups.

In a large bowl sift together flour, baking powder and salt. Cut in shortening until consistency resembles coarse crumbs. Stir in rolled oats.

In a small bowl combine egg, milk and brown sugar, beating well. Add to dry ingredients stirring until just moistened. Add raisins.

Spoon equally into paper baking cups. Combine sugar and cinnamon and sprinkle over muffins.

Bake 15 to 20 minutes or until top springs back when touched.

19

Finnish Pancakes

A delicious, different way to serve pancakes, from my sister,
Evelyn. It is a favorite dish enjoyed by her son, Craig Albrecht.

yield: 8 servings

4 **eggs**
1 **teaspoon vanilla**
1/3 **cup sugar**
2/3 **cup flour**
2 **cups milk**
4 **tablespoons butter**

Preheat oven to 425 degrees.

In a large bowl using an electric mixer, beat eggs until foamy.

Combine vanilla, sugar, flour and milk with eggs. Beat together until well blended.

Put butter in a 13 x 9-inch pan and place in oven. When butter is melted and bubbling, remove pan from oven and pour egg mixture into pan.

Return pan to oven and bake 30 minutes. Serve warm.

Aunt Irene's Pancakes

These pancakes are best served warm with
Door County maple syrup.
They are delicious!

yield: 6 to 8 pancakes

1 **egg**
1 **cup buttermilk**
1 **cup flour**
1 **teaspoon salt**
1/2 **teaspoon baking soda**

In a medium size bowl beat egg; stir in buttermilk. Beat in flour, salt and baking soda until smooth.

Grease griddle lightly with vegetable oil and place over medium heat. Pour a large spoonful of batter for each pancake on griddle. When bubbles form in center, flip pancakes and cook until golden brown on other side.

French Toast

*French toast was served in the hotel every other morning,
alternating with pancakes. It was best when made with
homemade bread and served with Door County maple syrup.
This recipe brings back a flood of memories.*

yield: 6-10 servings

6	eggs.
3/4	cup whole milk
1/2	teaspoon salt
1	teaspoon vanilla
2	tablespoons margarine or butter
6-10	slices of bread
1/4	cup powdered sugar

In a medium bowl using a fork or wire whisk, beat eggs. Beat
in milk, salt and vanilla.

In a large skillet over medium heat, melt margarine. Dip bread
into egg mixture, coating both sides. Cook bread on each side
2 or 3 minutes, or until golden brown. (Add more margarine if
needed.) Remove from pan and sprinkle with powdered sugar.

Nutritious Cereal for Quick Energy

yield: 10 cups

5 **cups rolled oats**
1 **cup sliced almonds**
1 **cup sesame seeds**
1 **cup sunflower seeds**
1 **cup shredded coconut**
1 **cup soy flour**
1 **cup powdered milk**
1 **cup wheat germ**
1/2 **cup water**
1 **cup honey**
1 **cup vegetable oil**
1 **cup raisins**

Preheat oven to 300 degrees.

In a large bowl combine oats, almonds, sesame seeds, sunflower seeds, coconut, flour, milk and wheat germ.

In a separate bowl stir together water, honey and oil until well mixed. Stir honey mixture into dry ingredients until evenly distributed. Spread mixture evenly onto 2 large baking sheets.

Bake, turning cereal every 10 minutes, until light brown, approximately 30 minutes. Remove from oven to cool. Stir in raisins. Store in airtight container.

Sour Cream Coffee Cake

*Every morning we served baskets of freshly baked coffee cake at
each table in the dining room. This coffee cake was a favorite
with the staff as well as the guests.*

yield: 24 slices

1 **cup sugar**	***Topping***
1/2 **cup butter (1 stick)**	1 **cup chopped pecans**
2 **eggs**	1/2 **cup sugar**
1 **teaspoon vanilla**	1 **teaspoon cinnamon**
2 **cups flour**	
1 **teaspoon baking soda**	
1/2 **teaspoon baking powder**	
1/2 **teaspoon salt**	
1 **cup sour cream**	

Preheat oven to 350 degrees. Grease a tube pan or an 8 x 8-inch
square pan.

In a large bowl, cream together sugar and butter; beat in eggs
and vanilla. Mix in flour, baking soda, baking powder, salt and
sour cream.

Combine pecans with sugar and cinnamon. Pour half of the
batter into prepared pan and top with half of the pecan-sugar
mixture. Cover with remaining batter. Top with remaining pecan-
sugar mixture.

Bake 30 to 35 minutes or until wooden pick inserted into center
comes out clean. Cool cake for 10 minutes. Loosen edges with a
long, sharp knife and carefully invert onto serving dish.

Poppy Seed Coffee Cake

*The hotel custom of serving baskets of warm coffee cake every morning
for breakfast presented my mother with a challenge. She had to come up
with something new and different for the guests and this is
one of the recipes she found. It soon became a favorite.*

yield: 24 slices

1/3	cup poppy seeds	2 1/2	cups flour
1	cup buttermilk	2	teaspoons baking powder
1/2	cup butter	1	teaspoon baking soda
1/2	cup sugar	1/2	teaspoon salt
3	eggs	1	teaspoon cinnamon
1	teaspoon vanilla	1/4	cup sugar

Soak poppy seeds in buttermilk in refrigerator at least 2 hours
or overnight.

Preheat oven to 350 degrees. Grease and flour tube pan.

In a large bowl, using electric mixer, cream butter and sugar until
fluffy. Add eggs and vanilla, continue beating until blended.

In a medium bowl stir together flour, baking powder, baking
soda and salt. Gradually add dry ingredients alternately with milk
mixture into the creamed mixture until well blended.

In a small bowl mix together cinnamon and sugar. Place half the
batter into tube pan. Sprinkle half of the sugar mixture over top
of batter. Cover with remaining batter. Top with remaining sugar
mixture.

Bake 1 hour. When cool, loosen edges with a long, sharp knife
and invert on serving dish.

Apple Nut Coffee Cake

*Smell the fragrance of freshly baked coffee cake,
hot from the oven. Our family enjoys making this cake
with Door County apples.*

yield: 15 to 18 servings

1 cup sugar	***Topping***
1/2 cup margarine	1/2 cup chopped nuts
2 eggs	1/2 cup brown sugar
1 teaspoon vanilla	1 teaspoon cinnamon
2 cups flour	2 tablespoons margarine,
1 teaspoon baking powder	melted
1 teaspoon baking soda	
1/4 teaspoon salt	
1 cup sour cream	
2 cups chopped apples	

Preheat oven to 350 degrees. Grease a 13 x 9-inch baking pan.

In a large bowl cream together sugar and margarine. Add eggs
and vanilla; beat well.

Combine flour, baking powder, baking soda and salt. Add to
creamed mixture alternately with sour cream, beginning and
ending with dry ingredients. Fold in apples.

Pour batter into prepared pan. In a medium bowl combine nuts,
brown sugar, cinnamon and margarine. Sprinkle topping over
batter.

Bake 35 to 40 minutes or until wooden pick inserted into center
comes out clean.

Moravian Sugar Cake

This cake is actually a traditional sweet bread made on special occasions in Moravian homes since colonial times. On Easter Sunday, many Moravian churches serve the cake after sunrise service. The Moravian Sugar Cake took first place in the bake-off one year at our local Scandinavian festival.

yield: 15 servings

1	package dry yeast	1	cup mashed potatoes
1	cup warm (110-115 degrees) water	3 3/4	cups flour, divided
2/3	cup sugar	*Topping*	
1/2	cup butter or margarine (1 stick)	1/2	cup butter (1 stick), melted
1	teaspoon salt	1 1/2	cups brown sugar
2	eggs, beaten	3	teaspoons cinnamon

Grease a 13 x 9-inch baking pan.

Dissolve yeast in water; let stand for 10 minutes. In a large bowl cream together sugar, butter and salt. Add eggs and potatoes. Add one cup of flour and beat until smooth. Stir in yeast mixture and enough of the remaining flour to make a soft dough.

Place in greased bowl, cover, and let rise for two hours or until doubled in size. Punch down and press dough into prepared pan.

With your thumb, make holes 2 inches apart on top of dough. Pour melted butter evenly into holes. Mix together brown sugar and cinnamon. Sprinkle over top. Let rise for 30 minutes more.

Preheat oven to 350 degrees.

Bake cake about 25 minutes or until top is golden brown.

Baked Eggs and Cheese

A favorite breakfast dish made by my sister, Evelyn Albrecht.
This recipe can be prepared the night before baking
and stored in the refrigerator.

yield: 12 to 15 servings

6	slices bread
	Butter
2	cups cubed ham
1	package (8 ounces) shredded Cheddar cheese
7	eggs, beaten
2 1/2	cups milk
1	green pepper, chopped
1	onion, chopped
8	slices bread, cubed
1/3	cup butter, melted
1/2	teaspoon paprika

Preheat oven to 350 degrees.

Butter bread slices on one side and remove crusts. Place bread, buttered side down, in a 13 x 9-inch pan.

In a large bowl mix together ham, cheese, beaten eggs, milk, green pepper and onion. Pour egg mixture over bread slices. Put cubed bread over top of egg mixture. Pour melted butter over bread cubes; sprinkle paprika on top.

Bake uncovered 1 hour. Serve warm.

Baked Breakfast Omelet

This recipe can be prepared the night before and stored in the refrigerator.

yield: 12 to 15 squares

1/4	**cup margarine (1/2 stick)**
4	**slices bread, cubed (3 cups)**
18	**eggs**
1	**cup sour cream**
1	**cup milk**
2	**teaspoons salt**
1/4	**teaspoon nutmeg**
1/4	**teaspoon pepper**
1/4	**cup flour**
1/4	**cup chopped green onions**
2	**cups shredded Cheddar cheese**
1	**cup shredded Swiss cheese**
11/2	**cups cubed ham**
1/2	**cup sliced mushrooms**

Preheat oven to 325 degrees.

Melt margarine. Coat bottom of a 13 x 9-inch baking pan with margarine; cover with bread cubes. Set aside.

In a large bowl beat eggs; add sour cream, milk, salt, nutmeg, pepper, flour, onions, cheeses, ham and mushrooms. Pour mixture evenly over bread cubes.

Bake 1 hour and 15 minutes or until top is brown and eggs are firm. Cut into squares and serve.

Laurel's Rice Pudding

*This is our very favorite pudding. We served it for breakfast,
on special occasions, and always on Christmas Eve.*

yield: 12 servings

1	cup rice
2	quarts milk (8 cups), divided
1	cup sugar, divided
1	teaspoon salt
5	eggs, beaten
1	teaspoon vanilla
1 1/2	teaspoons cinnamon

Preheat oven to 350 degrees. Grease a 13 x 9-inch pan.

In a double boiler combine rice, 4 cups of the milk, 1/3 cup of
sugar and salt. Cook until tender, about 20 minutes.

In a large saucepan over low heat, warm remaining 4 cups of
milk. In a large bowl combine warmed milk, eggs, vanilla and
remaining 2/3 cup of the sugar; add to rice mixture.

Pour into a 13 x 9-inch cake pan. Sprinkle cinnamon on top.
Bake 35 to 40 minutes or until wooden pick inserted into center
comes out clean. Serve either warm or cold.

Breads

White Bread

This is a family favorite which is enjoyed by guests as well.
It is a special treat when served warm from the oven.

yield: 2 loaves

2	packages dry yeast
11/2	cups warm (110-115 degrees) water
11/2	cups milk
1/4	cup sugar
11/2	teaspoons salt
4	tablespoons margarine
7	cups flour (approximately)

Grease two 9 x 5 x 3-inch loaf pans.

In a small bowl dissolve yeast in water; set aside. Scald milk; add sugar, salt and margarine. Pour milk mixture into large bowl; cool. Add yeast mixture stirring to combine. Add flour in small amounts until a soft dough forms. Knead on lightly floured surface or mix with dough hooks of electric mixer until smooth and elastic. Place in greased bowl. Cover and let rise until double in size, approximately 2 hours.

Punch down and divide dough in half. Form into 2 loaves and place into prepared pans. Let rise 1 hour.

Preheat oven to 400 degrees.

Bake 40 to 45 minutes. Remove from pans to cool.

Cool-Rise White Bread

This recipe was submitted by my sister, Grace Vernon,
who is the best bread and roll baker in the whole family.

yield: 2 loaves

1/2	cup water	2	tablespoons sugar
1 3/4	cups milk	1	tablespoon salt
2	packages dry yeast	6	cups flour
3	tablespoons margarine, melted		

Grease two 9 x 5 x 3-inch loaf pans.

In a medium saucepan warm together water and milk over low heat.

In a large bowl dissolve yeast into water-milk mixture. Add melted margarine, sugar and salt.

Add flour into mixture and mix thoroughly. Turn out onto lightly floured surface and knead until smooth and elastic, about 10 minutes. Cover with plastic wrap and let rest on floured surface for 20 minutes.

Punch down and divide dough into 2 equal portions. Form into loaves. Put into prepared pans. Brush tops with oil. Cover loosely with oiled waxed paper, then cover with plastic wrap. Put into refrigerator until double in size or overnight.

Preheat oven to 400 degrees.

Bake 30 to 40 minutes or until tops are brown and bottoms of loaves sound hollow when tapped. Remove loaves from pans and cool on rack.

Dinner Rolls

*We always served rolls with dinner and even had
a basket of "bollers" on the smorgasbord table along with
Norwegian Julekake coffee cake.*

yield: 3 dozen rolls

  1   **cup milk**
1/4   **cup sugar**
  1   **teaspoon salt**
1/4   **cup margarine** (1/2 **stick**)
  2   **packages dry yeast**
1/2   **cup warm** (110-115 **degrees**) **water**
  2   **eggs, beaten**
  6   **cups flour** (**approximately**), **divided**

Scald milk; put in large bowl. Stir in sugar, salt and margarine,
set aside to cool. Dissolve yeast in water. Let sit 10 minutes.

Add yeast to milk mixture. Add eggs and 2 cups of the flour; stir
well. Add enough remaining flour to form a soft dough. Turn onto
lightly floured surface; knead dough 8 minutes. Place in greased
bowl. Let rise until double in size.

Grease baking sheets. Punch dough down and form into 2-inch
round balls. Place on prepared baking sheet 2 inches apart and
let dough rise for 30 minutes.

Preheat oven to 375 degrees.

Bake 15 to 20 minutes until rolls are golden and bread springs
back when touched.

Laurel's Caramel Rolls

My mother often made these luscious caramel rolls for our family.

yield: about 16 rolls

1 package dry yeast	***Caramel Pecan Mixture***
1/4 cup warm	1 cup brown sugar
(110-115 degrees) water	2 tablespoons butter or
1 cup milk	margarine
1/4 cup butter (1/2 stick)	1/4 cup corn syrup
1 teaspoon salt	3 tablespoons butter,
1/4 cup sugar	melted
2 eggs, beaten	1/2 cup pecans
31/2 cups flour, divided	1 teaspoon cinnamon
	1/4 cup sugar

Dissolve yeast in water; set aside. Scald milk, pour into a large bowl. Add butter, salt and sugar mixing well. Cool. Add yeast mixture, eggs and 1 cup of the flour. Beat until smooth. Continue to add remaining 21/2 cups of the flour to form soft dough. Knead on lightly floured surface until smooth, about 10 minutes. Place in greased bowl; cover and let rise until double in size, about 2 hours.

Grease a 13 x 9-inch baking pan.

Mix together brown sugar, butter and corn syrup. Sprinkle into bottom of prepared pan evenly covering entire surface. Heat in oven until melted. Spread pecans over caramel mixture.

Roll dough on floured surface into a rectangle. Brush with melted butter. Combine cinnamon and sugar and sprinkle evenly over the top. Roll as for a jelly roll, then slice into 1-inch slices. Place slices over caramel mixture in pan. Cover rolls and let rise for 30 minutes.

Preheat oven to 375 degrees. Bake 25 to 30 minutes. Cool for 15 minutes. Place a baking sheet over pan and invert rolls so caramel-pecan mixture is the topping.

Norwegian Julekake Bread

*We served this favorite Christmas coffee cake at our smorgasbord table.
Today it's enjoyed by the family on Christmas eve.*

yield: 1 round loaf

1 cup milk	***Butter Frosting***
1/2 cup butter (1 stick)	2 cups powdered sugar
1/2 cup sugar	2 tablespoons whole milk
1/2 teaspoon salt	1 tablespoon butter,
1 egg, beaten	melted
3/4 cup raisins	1 teaspoon vanilla
2 packages dry yeast	
1/4 cup warm (110-115 degrees) water	
3 cups flour	
2/3 cup rolled oats	
1/2 teaspoon cardamom	

Scald milk; pour into a large bowl. Stir in butter, sugar, salt, egg
and raisins. Set aside to cool.

Dissolve yeast in water, let sit 10 minutes. Add to cooled milk
mixture. Add flour, oats and cardamom. Knead on lightly floured
surface. Place in greased bowl and let rise 1 hour. Punch down.

Grease a 9-inch round pan; add dough. Let rise again, about 1 1/2
hours or until double in size. Preheat oven to 350 degrees. Bake
45 minutes.

To make frosting, in a small bowl combine powdered sugar,
milk, butter and vanilla; whisk until well blended and of spreading consistency. Spread top of Julekake with frosting.

Harry's Lefse Bread

*The last time Harry Trodahl (my mother's cousin) made lefse for us,
we were at his sister's cottage, across the bay in Cedar River, Michigan.
He baked it right on top of the old wood stove, as we stood around
the kitchen. We ate it warm from the stove. It was the best lefse we ever
tasted. Lefse can be spread with butter and rolled up. It is good with
sugar and cinnamon sprinkled on top, or with jam.*

yield: 12 pieces

2	**cups water**
1/4	**pound margarine or butter (1 stick)**
1	**teaspoon salt**
1	**pint half-and-half**
4	**cups dry instant mashed potatoes**
3	**cups flour**

Lightly dust working surface with flour.

In a large saucepan boil water. Add margarine, salt and half-and-half. Stir in flaked potatoes with a wire whisk. Cool completely.

Add flour to cooled potato mixture and mix well. Roll into 12 small balls. On prepared surface, using a rolling pin, roll balls out to resemble a pie crust.

Lightly grease an electric grill or pancake griddle. Fry pieces over medium heat until brown spots appear. Turn and fry until bottom side is lightly browned.

Remove from heat and cool between pieces of waxed paper.

Banana Muffins

*Here is a favorite recipe baked by my granddaughter, Laurel Cox,
who is named after her great-grandmother, Laurel Knudson.
She carries on the family tradition of a love for baking.*

yield: 12 muffins

1	cup flour
1/2	cup sugar
21/2	teaspoons baking powder
1/4	teaspoon baking soda
1/2	teaspoon salt
3/4	cup rolled oats
1/4	cup vegetable oil
1	egg, beaten
1/2	cup milk
1/2	cup mashed banana

Preheat oven to 400 degrees. Line 12-cup muffin tin with paper
baking cups.

Sift flour, sugar, baking powder, baking soda and salt into bowl.
Stir in oats. Add oil, egg, milk and banana; stir until just moistened.

Fill baking cups 2/3 full. Bake 20 minutes. Serve warm.

Banana Bread Treat

yield: 1 loaf

1 3/4 cups flour
2 teaspoons baking powder
1/4 teaspoon baking soda
3/4 teaspoon salt
1/4 cup margarine (1/2 stick)
2/3 cup sugar
2 eggs
1 cup mashed bananas
(approximately 2 large bananas)
1/2 cup chopped pecans

Preheat oven to 350 degrees. Grease and flour a 9 x 5 x 3-inch loaf pan.

In a medium bowl mix flour, baking powder, baking soda and salt.

In a separate bowl cream margarine and sugar until light and fluffy. Add eggs one at a time, beating well after each addition. Add bananas and mix.

Gradually add flour mixture, blending well. Stir in pecans. Pour into prepared pan.

Bake 50 to 60 minutes or until wooden pick inserted into center comes out clean. Bread is delicious served warm or cool.

Carrot Bread

yield: loaf

2 **cups flour**
2 **teaspoons baking soda**
2 **teaspoons cinnamon**
1/2 **teaspoon salt**
11/2 **cups sugar**
1/2 **cup shredded coconut, optional**
1/2 **cup chopped nuts**
3 **eggs, beaten**
1 **cup vegetable oil**
1 **teaspoon vanilla**
2 **cups grated carrots**

Preheat oven to 350 degrees. Grease and flour a 9 x 5 x 3-inch loaf pan.

Mix flour, baking soda, cinnamon, salt and sugar in a medium bowl. Add coconut and nuts; mix well. Add eggs, oil, vanilla and carrots. Beat until smooth. Pour batter into prepared pan. Let stand for 20 minutes.

Bake 50 minutes or until wooden pick inserted into center comes out clean.

Pineapple Zucchini Bread

*This moist, spicy, delicious bread is one of my sister's, Evelyn Albrecht's,
favorite recipes. If I have zucchini left in the late summer,
this is the bread I bake.*

yield: 2 loaves

3 eggs	2 teaspoons baking soda
1 cup vegetable oil	1/2 teaspoon baking powder
2 cups sugar	3/4 teaspoon nutmeg
2 teaspoons vanilla	1 teaspoon salt
2 cups shredded zucchini	2 teaspoons cinnamon
1 can (8 ounces) crushed	1 cup raisins
pineapple, drained	1 cup nuts, chopped
3 cups flour	

Preheat oven to 350 degrees. Grease and flour two 9 x 5 x 3-inch
loaf pans.

In a large mixing bowl using an electric mixer, beat together
eggs, oil, sugar and vanilla until thick and foamy. Stir in zucchini
and pineapple.

In a separate bowl combine flour, baking soda, baking powder,
nutmeg, salt, cinnamon, raisins and nuts. Mix flour mixture into
zucchini-pineapple mixture; blend well.

Pour mixture evenly into prepared loaf pans. Bake 1 hour or
until wooden pick inserted into center comes out clean. Let bread
cool in pans before removing.

Store in plastic bags when completely cooled.

Cranberry Orange Bread

My sister, Grace Vernon, always bakes small loaves of this bread at Christmastime, to give as gifts. The cranberries give it a festive look. However, this bread is good any time of the year.

yield: 1 loaf

2	cups flour
11/2	teaspoons baking powder
1/2	teaspoon salt
1	cup sugar
1/4	cup (1/2 stick) margarine, softened
	Juice of 1 orange (approximately 1/4 cup)
	Grated zest of 1 orange (approximately 2 teaspoons)
3/4	cup water
1	egg, beaten
11/2	cups fresh cranberries

Preheat oven to 350 degrees. Grease a 9 x 5 x 3-inch loaf pan.

In a large bowl stir together flour, baking powder, salt and sugar. Add margarine, juice of orange, zest, water and egg. Mix thoroughly.

Cut cranberries in half and fold into dough. Pour into prepared pan.

Bake 1 hour or until wooden pick inserted into center comes out clean. Cool in pan before removing.

Cottage Cheese Dill Bread

*This bread recipe always turns out and is low calorie,
according to my sister, Grace Vernon. When she makes it for company
she gets rave reviews.*

yield: 1 round loaf

1	package dry yeast	1	tablespoon onion flakes
1/4	cup warm (110-115 degrees) water	1/4	teaspoon baking soda
2	tablespoons sugar	1	egg, beaten
1	teaspoon salt	1	cup cottage cheese
2	teaspoons dill weed	31/4	cups flour (approximately), divided

In a small bowl mix yeast in water.

In a saucepan, combine sugar, salt, dill weed, onion flakes, baking soda, egg and cottage cheese. Stir mixture over low heat until warm.

Pour the cottage cheese mixture into a large bowl while still warm. Add 1 cup flour; mixing well. Add yeast mixture and mix. Add enough remaining flour for medium stiff dough.

Turn dough out onto lightly floured surface. Knead dough for 10 minutes or until smooth. (The dough will be sticky at first.) Put into greased bowl, cover and let rise until double in size, about 11/2 hours.

Preheat oven to 375 degrees. Grease a round casserole dish. Punch dough down and shape into a round loaf. Place dough in dish.

Bake 35 to 40 minutes, until top is golden brown. Remove from dish to a board or rack to cool.

Diane's Baking Powder Biscuits

My daughter, Diane Jacobson, serves these biscuits hot with plenty of butter or with strawberries as strawberry shortcake. (Sprinkle 1/2 cup sugar over 1 quart of strawberries in a large bowl—ready to use in an hour) MMMMMM-Good!

yield: 12 biscuits

2 **cups sifted all-purpose flour**
3 **teaspoons baking powder**
1 **teaspoon salt**
1/3 **cup shortening**
3/4 **cup milk**
1/4 **cup cream**

Preheat oven to 450 degrees.

Sift flour, baking powder, and salt into a mixing bowl. Cut in shortening with pastry blender until the mixture is fine. Make a well in the flour-shortening mixture and add milk all at once. Stir with a fork until dough is soft, not sticky.

Turn the dough out onto lightly floured surface. Knead or fold dough over gently, about six times. Pat dough to about 1/2-inch thickness. Using floured biscuit cutter, cut biscuits close together to save rerolling. Lift biscuits with a spatula placing onto ungreased baking sheet or inverted pan. (Place them 1 inch apart for crusty biscuits or close together for soft.) Brush biscuits with cream.

Bake 10 to 12 minutes or until golden brown.

Soups

Broccoli Cheese Soup

This recipe comes from Laurel's granddaughter, Janel Vernon,
who loves to serve this homemade soup with hot rolls.

yield: 4 servings

4	tablespoons butter
1/4	cup flour
1¹/4	cups chicken broth
1¹/4	cups milk
1/2	cup shredded Cheddar cheese
1/2	cup cooked chopped broccoli
3	slices American cheese
1/8	teaspoon salt
1/8	teaspoon pepper
	Croutons, for garnish

Melt butter in a large saucepan over low heat. Stir in flour until mixture is smooth. Cook 1 minute, stirring constantly. Gradually stir in broth and milk. Cook over medium heat stirring constantly until thickened and bubbly. Add Cheddar cheese, broccoli, American cheese, salt and pepper. Stir until cheese is well blended. Serve with croutons.

Cream of Broccoli Soup

yield: 4 to 6 servings

1 **bunch broccoli, finely chopped**
1 **chicken bouillon cube**
2 **tablespoons butter**
1 **stalk celery, chopped**
1 **small onion, chopped**
3 **tablespoons flour**
1 **teaspoon salt**
4 **cups milk**

Cook broccoli in water until tender, drain and set aside. Dissolve bouillon cube in 1/8 cup of boiling water. Set aside.

In a medium saucepan melt butter; add celery and onion and cook until tender. Add flour and salt, stirring with a wooden spoon until blended. Add milk a little at a time stirring to blend. Stir in broccoli and add bouillon mixture. Stir and simmer for about 1/2 hour or until flavors are blended. Serve hot.

Salmon Chowder

This recipe comes from the state of Washington, where Terri Vernon and her family live. We're so glad she shared this tasty chowder with us.

yield: 12 servings

6 slices bacon, diced	1/4 teaspoon pepper
1 1/2 cups diced celery	2 large salmon steaks,
1 cup chopped onion	cooked, boned and
3 cups diced potatoes	flaked, or 1 can
2 cans (10 3/4 ounces	(15 ounces) salmon
each) chicken broth	3 tablespoons flour
1 1/2 teaspoons salt	2 cups milk, divided
1/2 teaspoon paprika	1 cup cream
1/2 teaspoon dried thyme	
or dill weed	

In a dutch oven, partially cook bacon; drain. Add celery, onion and potatoes. Cook, stirring occasionally, until tender. Add chicken broth, salt, paprika, thyme or dill and pepper. Bring to a boil. Reduce heat; add salmon and simmer for 15 minutes.

Blend flour into 1/4 cup of the milk to make a paste. Pour remaining 1 3/4 cups of the milk and cream into dutch oven. Quickly stir in flour mixture. Cook, stirring frequently, until heated through and lightly thickened, about 15 minutes. Serve hot.

Diane's Potato Cheese Soup

Here is a favorite recipe made by my daughter, Diane, for her family.
Since all three of her daughters like potatoes and cheese,
they enjoy eating this soup while also having a healthy meal.

yield: 4 to 6 servings

1	pound potatoes	1/8	teaspoon ground pepper
2	cups water	4	ounces sharp cheddar
1/2	cup chopped carrot		cheese, shredded
1/2	cup chopped celery	1	cup minced fresh parsley
1/2	cup chopped onion		
2	teaspoons chicken		
	bouillon granules		

Peel and cut potatoes into 1/2-inch cubes so there is approximately 2 cups.

Into a large saucepan, place potatoes, water, carrot, celery, onion, bouillon granules and pepper. Over medium-high heat, bring to a boil; reduce heat to low, cover and simmer for 25 minutes or until vegetables are tender.

Place half of the ingredients at a time in a blender or food processor bowl; cover. Blend or process until smooth. Return mixture to saucepan. Add cheese. Cook, stirring over medium heat until cheese melts. To serve, sprinkle with parsley.

All Day Split-Pea Soup

My daughter, Diane, likes to make soups in her crock pot.
After you have all the ingredients put together you can
do other things while it cooks away. It is worth waiting for.

yield: 8 to 10 cups

1	package (16 ounces) split green peas
5-7	cups water
1-1 1/2	pounds smoked pork hock
2	cups diced potatoes
1 1/2	cups chopped onion
1	cup cubed celery
1	cup sliced carrot
1	clove garlic, crushed
1	tablespoon salt
1/4	teaspoon pepper
1/4	teaspoon Tabasco sauce

Rinse peas under cold running water.

In a large bowl, combine all ingredients. Place in a slow cooker
or crock pot. Cook on proper setting according to manufacturer's
directions for 6 to 8 hours.

Just before serving, remove hock. Cut pork from bone into bite-
size pieces. Return meat to soup and serve.

Vegetable-Beef Soup

yield: 6 to 8 servings

  1 **beef bouillon cube**
  1 **pound ground beef**
  1 **small onion, chopped**
  1 **tablespoon butter**
  1 **teaspoon salt**
1/4 **teaspoon pepper**
  1 **can (14 1/2 ounces) tomatoes**
  1 **can (10 3/4 ounces) consommé**
  2 **cups water**
  2 **cups coarsely diced celery**
  2 **cups diced carrots**
  1 **package frozen peas**
1/4 **cup barley**
1/2 **teaspoon sugar**

Dissolve bouillon cube in 1 cup of boiling water.

In a medium skillet brown beef and onion in butter with salt and pepper. Drain; transfer mixture to a large saucepan. Add tomatoes, consommé, water and bouillon mixture. Stir in celery, carrots, peas, barley and sugar. Cook covered for 45 minutes to 1 hour.

Bean Soup

Serve Bean Soup in warmed soup bowls with crackers.

yield: 6 to 8 servings

2	cups dry navy beans
6	cups water
1/2	cup chopped onion
1/2	cup chopped celery
2	potatoes, diced
1	teaspoon salt
1/4	teaspoon pepper
1	cup diced ham

Soak beans overnight in enough water to cover them. Drain beans. Combine beans and water and simmer in covered saucepan for 2 hours.

Stir in onion, celery, potatoes, salt, pepper and ham. Cover and simmer 1 hour. Do not let soup boil.

Chili

This favorite chili recipe is from my sister, Evelyn.
She lives in the big snow country and likes to serve this dish after an
afternoon of cross-country skiing. Serve with warm bread or rolls.

yield: 6 to 8 servings

1	**pound ground beef**
1	**green pepper, chopped**
2	**medium onions, chopped**
1/2	**teaspoon garlic salt**
1/4	**teaspoon seasoned salt**
1	**envelope chili mix**
1	**teaspoon chili powder**
1	**can (14 1/2 ounces) tomatoes**
2	**cans (15 ounces each) kidney beans**
4	**cups water**

In a large skillet brown beef; drain. Add pepper, onions, garlic salt, seasoned salt, chili mix and chili powder. Cook on medium heat for $\pi15$ minutes.

Stir in tomatoes and juice from can into meat mixture and simmer until well heated. Add beans and water and simmer 15 minutes longer.

Norwegian Fruit Soup

yield: 8 servings

1/2	pound pitted prunes
11/2	cups currants
11/2	cups raisins
21/2	cups diced apples (about 3 medium)
1/3	cup cooked rice
3	tablespoons tapioca
1/2	cup sugar
2	tablespoons lemon juice

In a large saucepan combine prunes, currants, raisins and apples with enough cold water to cover and bring to a boil. Allow mixture to simmer until fruit is soft, but not mushy, about 1 hour. Add cooked rice. Stir in tapioca; cook until mixture is clear.

Add sugar, cook 2 minutes. Set aside to cool. When mixture is cool, add lemon juice. Serve chilled.

Salads

Molded Tuna Salad

My mother, Laurel, always served this fish salad at our smorgasbord.
She doubled the recipe, and used a large fish mold.
When serving, she added a sliced green olive for the fish's eye.
Serve with additional mayonnaise and tuna if desired.

yield: 4 to 6 servings

1   package (3 ounces) lemon gelatin
1   cup boiling water
1/2 cup cold water
2   tablespoons lemon juice
1/2 cup mayonnaise
1/4 teaspoon salt
1   can (8 ounces) chunk-style tuna
3/4 cup chopped cucumber or celery
1/4 cup sliced green olives
2   tablespoons chopped pimento
1/2 teaspoon grated onion

In a medium bowl dissolve gelatin in boiling water. Stir in cold water, lemon juice, mayonnaise and salt. Put bowl in freezer. Quick chill until firm, 1 inch from edge of bowl, but soft in the center, about 15 minutes. Transfer mixture to a larger bowl and whip until fluffy.

Fold tuna, cucumber or celery, olives, pimento and onion into gelatin mixture. Pour into mold (a fish mold if you have one). Refrigerate until firm. Unmold onto serving platter.

Chicken Salad

yield: 6 to 8 servings

4 cups diced cooked chicken
2 cups sliced celery
1/2 cup pecans
1 can (20 ounces) pineapple chunks, drained
4 hard-boiled eggs, quartered
1 cup frozen peas, thawed
1 cup salad dressing
4 tablespoons lemon juice
1 tablespoon salt

In a large bowl, combine chicken, celery, pecans, pineapple, eggs and peas.

Blend salad dressing, lemon juice and salt in a medium bowl.

Add dressing mixture to chicken mixture and mix lightly. Chill before serving.

Carrot Salad

yield: 6 servings

1 **package (3 ounces) orange Jello**
1/2 **teaspoon salt**
1 **cup boiling water**
1 **can (8 ounces) crushed pineapple**
1 **tablespoon lemon juice**
1 **cup grated carrots**

In a medium pan dissolve Jello and salt in boiling water.

Add pineapple with juice, lemon juice and carrots. Pour into glass bowl or mold.

Chill about 1 hour in refrigerator before serving.

Carrots Marinade

yield: 8 to 10 servings

2 pounds carrots, peeled and sliced
1 large onion, chopped
1 green pepper, thinly sliced
1 can (10 3/4 ounces) tomato soup
3/4 cup sugar
1/2 cup vegetable oil
3/4 cup vinegar
1 teaspoon salt
1/2 teaspoon pepper

In a large saucepan, cook carrots until crisp-tender; drain. Combine carrots, onion and green pepper in a large glass bowl.

In a medium bowl, stir together tomato soup, sugar, oil, vinegar, salt and pepper until well blended. Pour sauce over vegetables and stir lightly.

Place bowl in refrigerator and chill for several hours before serving.

Evergreen Beach Coleslaw

yield: 6 cups

4 cups grated green cabbage
1/4 cup grated carrots
1/4 cup diced green pepper
2 tablespoons chopped fresh parsley
1 tablespoon grated onion

Dressing
4 strips bacon, crisply cooked
  and crumbled
2 tablespoons lemon juice
1 teaspoon salt
1/8 teaspoon pepper
2/3 cup mayonnaise

In a large bowl, mix together cabbage, carrots, green pepper, parsley, and onion. Chill in refrigerator until ready to add dressing.

In a separate small bowl, whisk together bacon, lemon juice, salt, pepper and mayonnaise. Chill until ready to serve. Pour over cabbage mixture and mix thoroughly.

Three Bean Salad

This salad looks good served in a pretty glass dish.

yield: 8 to 10 servings

1 can (14 1/2 ounces) green beans, drained
1 can (14 1/2 ounces) wax beans, drained
1 can (14 1/2 ounces) kidney beans,
    drained and rinsed
1/2 cup minced green pepper
1/2 cup sliced celery
1/2 cup thinly sliced onion

Dressing
1/2 cup vinegar
1/2 cup vegetable oil
3/4 cup sugar
1 teaspoon salt
1/2 teaspoon pepper

In a medium bowl toss together green, wax and kidney beans. Mix in green pepper, celery and onion.

In a large bowl, combine vinegar, vegetable oil, sugar, salt and pepper. Add bean mixture and toss lightly. Refrigerate 4 or 5 hours or overnight before serving to blend flavors.

Floyd's Creamy Cucumber Salad

When my dad, Floyd, was growing up, everyone had a garden, so he learned from his mother, Ella Knudson, how to prepare fresh vegetables from her garden. We enjoyed this recipe's fresh, crispy taste.

yield: 4 servings

1	large cucumber
1	cup sour cream
1	tablespoon chopped onion
3	tablespoons vinegar
1 1/2	teaspoons salt
1/8	teaspoon pepper

Peel cucumber. Run tines of fork lengthwise of cucumber; cut cucumber crosswise into thin slices.

Combine sour cream, onion, vinegar, salt and pepper and pour over cucumber. Refrigerate 30 minutes before serving.

Irene's Sauerkraut Salad

My aunt, Irene Knudson, served this favorite salad at family gatherings.
After selling Pisha's Restaurant in Sister Bay, she helped me
prepare breakfast for guests of the hotel.

yield: 6 to 8 servings

1 jar or plastic bag
    (32 ounces) sauerkraut
1 cup diced celery
1/2 green pepper, diced
1 onion, thinly sliced
1/4 teaspoon celery seed
1/2 cup salad oil
1/2 cup vinegar
11/2 cups sugar

Drain, rinse and chop sauerkraut. Place in a medium bowl and mix with celery, green pepper, onion and celery seed.

In a saucepan, mix salad oil, vinegar and sugar; heat until warm. Cool; pour over sauerkraut mixture. Refrigerate overnight before serving.

Sauerkraut salad keeps well for several days when refrigerated.

Vegetable Salad

*This pretty green and white salad is a recipe from my sister, Grace.
It's great for a buffet or summer picnic, and tastes crisp and crunchy.*

yield: 8 to 10 servings

    1 **bunch broccoli**
    1 **head cauliflower**
    1 **package (10 ounces) frozen peas**
    6 **green onions, chopped**
    2 **cups mayonnaise**
    1 **teaspoon salt**
    2 **tablespoons sugar**
    1 **cup sour cream**
  3/4 **teaspoon garlic salt**

Chop up broccoli and cauliflower; place in a large bowl. Thaw
peas by running water over them; drain and add to bowl. Add
onions and stir to mix.

In a separate bowl mix mayonnaise, salt, sugar, sour cream and
garlic salt. Pour over mixed vegetables. Refrigerate several hours
before serving.

Fruit Salad

yield: 6 to 8 servings

2 **cans (20 ounces each) chunk pineapple**
2 **cans (11 ounces each) mandarin oranges**
1 **large bunch green grapes**
3 **tablespoons Tang powder**
1 **package (3 ounces) instant vanilla pudding**
3 **bananas, optional**

Drain pineapple, reserving juice in separate bowl. Drain
mandarin oranges, discarding juice. Cut grapes in half. Mix fruit
together in a large bowl.

In a medium bowl, whisk together 1 cup of the reserved pineapple juice, Tang and vanilla pudding. Pour over fruit mixture
and stir until mixed. Chill in refrigerator.

Before serving, you may also add sliced bananas.

Mandarin Orange Salad

yield: 8 to 10 servings

2   **packages (3 ounces each) orange Jello**
1^{1/2}   **cups hot water**
1   **cup fresh or frozen orange juice**
1   **pint orange sherbet**
1   **can (9 1/2 ounces) crushed pineapple, drained**
1   **can (11 ounces) mandarin oranges, drained**

Dissolve Jello in water in a large bowl. Add orange juice and sherbet. Stir until well blended.

Let Jello and sherbet mixture stand in refrigerator until it begins to congeal, about 10 minutes then add pineapple and orange segments.

Pour Jello mixture into a mold or a pretty glass dish. Refrigerate 4 to 5 hours until firm.

Cranberry Orange Mold

yield: 10 to 12 servings

1   can (20 ounces) crushed pineapple
1   can (11 ounces) mandarin oranges
2   packages (3 ounces each)
     cherry or cranberry Jello
1/4   teaspoon salt
1/4   teaspoon cinnamon
     Dash of cloves
1   can (16 ounces) whole cranberry sauce

Drain juice of pineapple and mandarin oranges in a 2-cup measure, reserving fruit. Add enough water to the juice to make 2 cups full. Place liquid in a small saucepan and bring to a boil.

In the meantime, mix together Jello, salt, cinnamon and cloves in a large bowl. Stir in boiling liquid until Jello is dissolved. Add cranberry sauce and mix until blended. Fold in reserved pineapple and mandarin oranges. Chill until firm, about 4 hours.

Strawberry Jello

yield: 6 to 8 servings

1   package (6 ounces) strawberry Jello
1   cup boiling water
1   package (16 ounces) frozen strawberries
1   can (20 ounces) crushed pineapple
2   bananas
1   cup sour cream

In a large bowl, dissolve Jello with water. When Jello is dissolved, stir in frozen strawberries and pineapple. Mash bananas in a separate bowl, with a fork, then add to Jello mixture.

Pour half of the Jello mixture into a mold, or glass dish, and chill about 15 minutes in refrigerator until firm. Spread sour cream over chilled mixture, then pour remaining Jello over top. Return to refrigerator and chill until firm, about 3 or 4 hours.

To serve, loosen mold around edge and turn onto serving dish, or serve in glass bowl.

Lime Pear Salad

*This salad, remembered from hotel smorgasbords is still made
by my daughter, Shelley Cox, for holidays. Its smooth, creamy taste
makes it a favorite of the grandchildren.*

yield: 6 to 8 servings

   1 **can (15 ounces) pears**
   1 **package (3 ounces) lime Jello**
   1 **package (3 ounces) cream cheese**
   2 **cups whipped topping or whipped cream**

Drain can of pears into a medium saucepan and bring juice to a
boil. (Do not add pears at this time.) Add lime Jello and dissolve.

In a large bowl with electric mixer, whip cream cheese until
fluffy. Add Jello mixture to cream cheese and mix.

In a small bowl with electric mixer on low, mash pears. Add
pears to the Jello-cream cheese mixture. Fold in whipped topping
or whipped cream. Pour into a mold and refrigerate until set,
about 4 hours.

Jello Bars

This gelatin recipe is a favorite of my youngest granddaughter,
Karin Jacobson. She and her mom make it often for birthday
parties, picnics and potluck suppers. Small children love these.

yield: 12 to 14 servings

3 **boxes (3 ounces each) flavored gelatin**
4 **envelopes (1/4 ounce each) unflavored gelatin**
4 **cups water**

In a large bowl, mix together flavored gelatin and unflavored
gelatin.

Boil water. Pour boiling water into gelatin. Stir for 2 minutes
until dissolved.

Pour into a 13 x 9-inch pan or two heart-shaped pans lightly
sprayed with cooking spray. Chill 2 hours. Cut into small squares.
Or, interesting shapes can be made by using different sized cookie
cutters.

Side & Main Dishes

Vidalia Onion Pie

yield: 6 servings

1 cup crushed saltine crackers
(about 16 crackers)
5 tablespoons butter
2 1/2 cups sliced vidalia onions
2 1/2 tablespoons vegetable oil
3/4 cup milk
2 eggs, beaten
Salt and pepper, to taste
1/4 cup grated sharp Cheddar cheese

Preheat oven to 350 degrees.

Put crushed crackers in a 9-inch pie plate. In a small pan melt butter and pour over crackers. Bake 8 minutes.

In a skillet sauté onions in oil until transparent.

In a medium bowl combine milk, eggs, salt and pepper to taste.

Put onions in pie crust, pour egg mixture over onions and top with cheese.

Bake 45 minutes.

Zucchini Pie

When my dad gave us zucchini from his garden, my daughter Shelley liked for me to make this dish for dinner served in a casserole dish.

yield: 6 to 8 servings

4 cups sliced zucchini	1/4 teaspoon black pepper
1 cup chopped onions	1/4 teaspoon garlic powder
1/2 cup butter (1 stick)	1/4 teaspoon dried basil
1/2 cup fresh chopped parsley or 2 teaspoons parsley flakes	1/4 teaspoon dried oregano
	2 eggs, beaten
1/2 teaspoon salt	2 cups grated Cheddar cheese

Preheat oven to 375 degrees. Grease a 2-quart casserole dish.

In a skillet, sauté zucchini and onions in butter for 10 minutes. Add parsley, salt, pepper, garlic powder, basil and oregano. Stir to combine.

Spoon mixture into prepared dish. Pour eggs over top and sprinkle evenly with cheese.

Bake 10 minutes. Cover with aluminum foil and bake an additional 10 minutes.

Baked Beans

My daughter, Diane Jacobson, began making these baked beans for family potluck picnics. They were so well received, she continues to bake them for all our family get-togethers.

yield: 8 to 10 servings

    1 **large can (55 ounces) baked beans**
    1 **small can (16 ounces) baked beans**
    1 **can (16 ounces) kidney beans**
    1 **can (15 1/2 ounces) butter beans**
    1 **onion, chopped**
 3/4 **pound bacon**
 1/2 **cup ketchup**
 1/2 **cup brown sugar**
    1 **cup Cheddar cheese, divided**

Preheat oven to 350 degrees.

Combine baked beans, kidney beans, butter beans and onion in a casserole dish.

Crisply fry bacon, crumble and add to bean mixture. Add ketchup, brown sugar, and 1/2 cup of cheese. Stir to mix. Sprinkle remaining cheese on top. Bake 1 hour.

Rice and Beans

This is a tasty vegetarian dish from my sister, Evelyn Albrecht.
It was also enjoyed by our Brazilian exchange students.

yield: 4 to 6 servings

1 cup rice
2 cups black beans
1 bay leaf
3 tablespoon vegetable oil
1 teaspoon salt
1/4 teaspoon black pepper
1 clove garlic
1/4 teaspoon curry powder
1 tablespoon dried oregano

1/2 teaspoon cumin
1/2 cup chopped onion
1/3 cup chopped red pepper
2 teaspoons oil
1 tablespoon Worcestershire
    sauce
1/2 teaspoon Tabasco sauce
1 teaspoon steak sauce

In a medium saucepan prepare rice according to directions on box; set aside.

In a large saucepan place black beans in enough water to cover. Add bay leaf, oil, salt, pepper, garlic and curry. Cook over medium heat until beans are soft, about 2 1/2 to 3 hours. When done, remove bay leaf and add oregano and cumin.

In a skillet, sauté onion and red pepper in oil until soft. Add Worcestershire, Tabasco and steak sauce.

In a large casserole dish combine rice and beans; serve immediately.

Spinach Rice Casserole

This great-tasting casserole dish is a favorite of Laurel's granddaughter, Melissa Staley. An easy-to-make main dish to serve for family or company.

yield: 4 to 6 servings

10	ounces frozen chopped spinach
1	onion, chopped
2	teaspoons minced garlic
1	cup sliced fresh mushrooms
1	cup sliced zucchini
2	teaspoons dried oregano
1	tablespoon olive oil
1	cup lowfat spaghetti sauce
1	cup lowfat ricotta cheese
2	cups cooked brown rice
1/4	cup grated Parmesan cheese

Preheat oven to 350 degrees. Grease a 13 x 9-inch baking pan.

Defrost and drain spinach; set aside.

Sauté onion, garlic, mushrooms, zucchini, oregano and olive oil in a skillet.

In a large bowl combine spinach, onion mixture, spaghetti sauce, ricotta cheese and rice; mix well.

Place mixture into prepared pan. Sprinkle cheese evenly over top of casserole and bake 30 minutes.

Vegetable Lasagna

yield: 8 to 10 servings

9 uncooked lasagna
  noodles
3 tablespoons margarine
1/2 cup chopped onion
1/2 cup chopped celery
1 can (28 ounces)
  chopped tomatoes
1 can (6 ounces) tomato
  paste
1/2 cup water

1/2 tablespoon dried basil
  leaves
1/2 teaspoon sugar
1/2 teaspoon salt
1/4 teaspoon pepper
1 can (16 ounces) mixed
  vegetables, drained
4 cups shredded
  mozzarella cheese

Prepare lasagna noodles according to package directions. Drain and set aside. Grease a 13 x 9-inch baking pan.

Preheat oven to 350 degrees.

In a large saucepan, melt margarine, add onion and celery and cook until tender. Stir in tomatoes, tomato paste, water, basil, sugar, salt and pepper. Bring to a boil, reduce heat and simmer for 15 minutes.

In prepared pan assemble lasagna in layers alternating lasagna noodles, canned vegetables, sauce mixture and cheese, using 1/3 of each for each layer.

Bake 30 to 40 minutes until hot and bubbly. Remove from oven and let stand for 10 minutes before cutting into squares.

German Potato Salad

We had a German cook at the time we were serving smorgasbord, and she liked to add this potato dish to the Scandinavian table.

yield: 8 to 10 servings

12	potatoes, cooked
3	hard-boiled eggs, chopped
1	cup chopped onion
1/4	pound bacon, diced
2	tablespoons butter
1/4	cup flour
1/2	cup vinegar
1/2	cup water
1/2	cup sugar
1/2	teaspoon salt

Cut potatoes in bite-size pieces into a large bowl. Add eggs and onion.

Fry bacon; drain and add to potato mixture.

In a saucepan, melt butter over medium heat and stir in flour; do not brown. Add vinegar, water, sugar and salt. Reduce heat and cook until thickened. Pour over potato mixture. Serve warm.

Quiche

This classy cheese pie recipe is often baked by my sister Grace.
She frequently serves it for lunch, Sunday brunch and Christmas morning.

yield: 6 servings

1 **pie shell (9 inches), unbaked**
1 **cup crumbled, crisply cooked bacon**
    or cubed ham
1 **cup shredded Swiss cheese**
6 **eggs**
1 **cup half-and-half or whipping cream**
1/2 **teaspoon salt**
1/4 **teaspoon pepper**

Preheat oven to 375 degrees.

Over the bottom of pie shell sprinkle crumbled bacon or cubed ham and cheese.

In a medium bowl, combine eggs, half-and-half, salt and pepper; beat until well blended. Pour over bacon and cheese in pie shell.

Bake 35 to 40 minutes, until the center is set. Turn off heat, leaving pie in oven for 10 minutes. Remove from oven and serve immediately.

Chicken Breasts

*I find this an easy way to make chicken,
and it always tastes elegant. Serve with rice.*

yield: 8 servings

4 **boneless, skinless chicken breasts**
8 **slices ham**
8 **slices Swiss cheese**
2 **cans (10 3/4 ounces each)
   cream of mushroom soup**

Preheat oven to 325 degrees.

Cut each chicken breast in half, removing extra fat. Wrap a
slice of ham around each half and place breasts close together in a
shallow baking dish. Place slices of Swiss cheese over chicken and
ham. Carefully spoon cream of mushroom soup over top.

Bake 1 hour.

Floyd's Baked Chicken

*Floyd's baked chicken was his pride and joy.
He would serve it at smorgasbord and later at family gatherings
every Sunday. He loved to tell anyone who would ask how to make it.*

yield: 6 to 8 servings

2	**cups flour**
1	**teaspoon salt**
1/8	**teaspoon pepper**
2	**chickens, cut in pieces**
11/2	**onions, chopped**
2	**stalks celery, chopped**
	Paprika
2	**chicken bouillon cubes**

Preheat oven to 350 degrees. Put flour, salt and pepper in a medium bowl. Coat each piece of chicken in mixture.

Cover bottom of a 13 x 9-inch pan with onions and celery. Set each piece of chicken on end, rather than flat, in pan. Shake paprika on each piece.

Boil 2 cups of water with bouillon cubes. Add to pan of chicken. Bake 45 minutes. Cover with aluminum foil and bake 30 to 45 minutes longer.

Floyd's Chicken Liver Loaf

*This was served on our smorgasbord table and
was a great favorite of guests.*

yield: 8 to 10 servings

1 **pound chicken livers, chopped**
1/4 **cup butter (1/2 stick)**
1/2 **teaspoon salt**
1 **medium onion, chopped**
1 **tablespoon dried parsley**
2 **hard-boiled eggs**
1 **package (3 ounces) cream cheese**
1 **tablespoon mayonnaise**

Combine chicken livers, butter, salt, onion and parsley in a
saucepan. Cover and simmer 10 minutes.

Purée mixture with hard-boiled eggs in a blender or a meat
grinder or press through a sieve.

In a medium bowl, whip together cream cheese and mayonnaise.
Add liver mixture; mix well. Chill in loaf pan or mold. Serve with
crackers.

Turkey Casserole

yield: 4 servings

1 **package (10 ounces) frozen,**
 chopped broccoli
3 **cups chopped, cooked turkey**
1 **can (10 3/4 ounces)**
 cream of mushroom soup
1/2 **cup milk**
1/2 **cup mayonnaise**
1/2 **cup Cheddar cheese**
1/4 **cup cooking wine**
1/4 **teaspoon garlic salt**
 Chinese noodles, optional

Preheat oven to 350 degrees.

Cook broccoli according to package instructions. Combine broccoli and turkey in a casserole dish. (If you like, you can add 2 sliced hard-boiled eggs.)

Heat together in a saucepan soup, milk, mayonnaise, cheese, wine and garlic salt. Pour sauce over turkey and broccoli. Top with Chinese noodles or leave plain.

Bake 30 minutes or until sauce is bubbly.

Door County Baked Whitefish

Every night of the week we served a special entree.
Baked whitefish was served every Friday night. It was so popular with
guests we began serving it on Tuesday nights also.

yield: 4 servings

4   **whitefish fillets,**
     6 to 8 ounces each
1   **onion, sliced**
2   **teaspoons salt**
1   **teaspoon paprika**
1   **cup whole milk**
     Lemons, for garnish

Preheat oven to 375 degrees. Line a 13 x 9-inch baking pan with aluminum foil.

Place fillets in pan skin-side down. Place onion slices over fish. Season with salt and paprika. Pour milk into pan just around bottom of fish, not on top.

Bake 40 to 45 minutes. Serve with lemon on the side.

Ham Ring with Cherry Sauce

This ham dish is great served with hot Door County cherry sauce.
My daughters and I often serve this dish when we have dinner guests.

yield: 6 to 8 servings

1 pound uncooked or cured ground ham	*Hot Cherry Sauce*
1 pound ground pork	1 can (16 ounces) pitted tart cherries (2 1/4 cups)
2 eggs, beaten	1/2 cup sugar
1 1/2 cups wheat flakes cereal	2 tablespoons cornstarch
1/2 cup milk	1/4 teaspoon cloves
1/4 cup brown sugar	
1 teaspoon mustard	
1/4 teaspoon cloves	

Preheat oven to 350 degrees. Lightly grease a ring mold or a
9 x 5 x 3-inch loaf pan.

In a large bowl using an electric mixer, combine ham, pork, eggs,
wheat flakes and milk; mix well. Pat mixture into prepared mold
or pan.

In a small bowl combine brown sugar, mustard and cloves;
spread on top of meat. Bake 1 hour for mold and 1 1/2 hours for
pan. Remove from oven, drain and invert onto platter.

Drain cherries, reserving liquid. In a small saucepan mix
together sugar, cornstarch and cloves. Gradually stir in cherry
liquid. Cook, stirring constantly until mixture boils and is thick.
Add cherries.

Serve hot cherry sauce in a bowl alongside ham platter.

Meat Loaf

This is a favorite meat loaf recipe of Evelyn's.
It is a delicious meat dish that I remember having for dinner
at the hotel, as well as for family dinners.

yield: 8 servings

1 1/2 **cups tomato juice**
1 **egg, beaten**
3/4 **cup rolled oats**
1 **teaspoon salt**
1/4 **teaspoon pepper**
1/4 **cup chopped onion**
2 **pounds lean ground beef**

Preheat oven to 350 degrees.

Combine tomato juice, egg, oats, salt, pepper and onion in a large mixing bowl; mix well. Add ground beef and mix lightly but thoroughly.

Press into a 9 x 5 x 3-inch loaf pan and bake 1 hour. Let stand 5 minutes before slicing to serve.

Norwegian Meatballs

Floyd made Norwegian meatballs every Tuesday and Saturday for our smorgasbord. They were so good that it was hard to keep the bowl full. Our favorite was to serve them with boiled potatoes.

yield: 6 to 8 servings

1 **pound ground round**
1 **pound ground pork**
1 **cup bread crumbs**
1/2 **cup milk**
1 **egg, beaten**
1/4 **onion, chopped**
1 **teaspoon salt**
1/4 **teaspoon pepper**
1 **teaspoon nutmeg**
1 **teaspoon allspice**
2 **tablespoons margarine**
2 **tablespoons flour**
1 **can (10 1/2 ounces)**
 consommé or beef broth

Combine ground round, ground pork, bread crumbs, milk, egg, onion, salt, pepper, nutmeg and allspice in a medium bowl. Mix well. Form into 1 1/2-inch balls.

Heat skillet on medium and melt margarine. Add meatballs and brown slowly, about 30 minutes, turning as meat browns. Remove meatballs from skillet; set aside.

Add flour to skillet and blend. Add consommé or beef broth. Cook until thickened over medium heat, about 20 minutes. Return meatballs to skillet. Simmer for 15 minutes. Serve hot.

Beef Stew

yield: 6 servings

2 pounds beef stew meat,
cut in 1-inch cubes
1 medium onion, quartered
2 stalks celery, diced
4 potatoes, cut in chunks
6 carrots, diced
2 teaspoons salt
3 tablespoons tapioca
1 tablespoon sugar
1 can (8 ounces) tomato sauce
1 cup water

Preheat oven to 275 degrees.

Mix beef, onion, celery, potatoes and carrots in a large casserole dish or pan.

Blend salt, tapioca and sugar in a medium bowl. Stir in tomato sauce and water. Pour mixture over beef and vegetables.

Cover pan and bake 4 hours.

New England Boiled Dinner

yield: 8 servings

3 **pounds corned beef**
2 **cloves garlic, minced**
2 **bay leaves**
8 **new potatoes**
4 **carrots, quartered**
2 **medium onions, quartered**
1 **head cabbage, cut into wedges**

In a large saucepan, cover meat with cold water. Add garlic and bay leaves. Bring to a boil; cover and reduce heat, cooking slowly for 3 hours.

Remove meat to cool. Add potatoes, carrots and onions to pan. Cover and cook over medium heat for 15 minutes. Add cabbage; cover and cook an additional 15 to 20 minutes.

Cut meat into bite-size pieces and return to pan; heat thoroughly. Drain meat and vegetables and arrange on serving dish.

Sour Cream Enchiladas

This recipe is a favorite of Laurel's granddaughter,
Annette Odle, who lives with her family out west.

yield: 8 to 10 servings

 2 **pounds ground beef**
 1 **small onion, chopped**
 1 **can (10 3/4 ounces) cream of mushroom soup**
 1 **can (10 3/4 ounces) cream of chicken soup**
 1 **pint sour cream**
1 1/2 **cups shredded Cheddar cheese**
10 **flour tortillas (8 inches round)**

Preheat oven to 350 degrees.

In a large skillet over medium heat, brown ground beef and
onion; drain. Set aside.

In a medium bowl mix together cream of mushroom soup,
cream of chicken soup, sour cream and cheese. Spread half of the
soup mixture on the bottom of a 13 x 9-inch pan.

Spoon approximately 1/4 cup ground beef into tortillas.
Roll up each one and place on top of soup mixture. Spread
remaining soup mixture over top of tortillas. Bake 1 hour.

Desserts

Rhubarb Crumble

My dad was an avid gardener, so of course he had a rhubarb patch in the spring. He enjoyed eating plain rhubarb sauce, but mother liked baking rhubarb pies and tortes. Her friend, Dorothy, gave her this delicious recipe to bake for the hotel. It may be served plain or with whipped cream.

yield: 9 servings

3	**cups chopped rhubarb**
2	**tablespoons orange juice**
1/2	**cup sugar**
1/4	**teaspoon cinnamon**
1	**tablespoon butter**
1/4	**cup shortening, melted**
1	**cup brown sugar**
2/3	**cup flour**
1/8	**teaspoon salt**
1/4	**teaspoon baking soda**
2/3	**cup rolled oats**

Preheat oven to 375 degrees. Grease a 9-inch square baking pan.

Arrange rhubarb in prepared pan. Sprinkle with orange juice, sugar, cinnamon and dot with butter.

In a small bowl combine shortening and brown sugar.

In a medium bowl stir together flour, salt, baking soda and oats. Blend brown sugar mixture into flour mixture until well mixed. Spread over rhubarb.

Bake 40 minutes.

Apple Crisp

Fall is a wonderful time for apple desserts.
My sister, Evelyn Albrecht, shared this recipe with the family
several years ago. It's our favorite and one we make many times,
especially in the fall. It may be served with ice cream,
cheese or whipped topping.

yield: 12 to 15 servings

1   cup brown sugar
2   cups flour
1/2   cup rolled oats
3/4   cup shortening
2   teaspoons cinnamon
1   teaspoon salt
9   cups apples, peeled and sliced
     (about 10 medium apples)
11/8   cup sugar, divided
1   tablespoon cornstarch
1   cup water

Preheat oven to 350 degrees.

In a large bowl mix together brown sugar, flour, oats, shortening, cinnamon and salt. Mix well.

Press half of the flour mixture into a 13 x 9-inch pan. Place apples over top of flour mixture. Sprinkle 1/8 cup of sugar over apples.

In a saucepan, cook cornstarch, remaining 1 cup of sugar and water until thickened. Pour over apples. Sprinkle the remaining half of the flour mixture on top of apples.

Bake 1 hour.

Pumpkin Torte

yield: 12 to 15 servings

Crust
24 graham cracker
squares, crushed
1/2 cup sugar
1/2 cup butter (1 stick),
melted

Filling
2 eggs
3/4 cup sugar
1 package (8 ounces)
cream cheese, softened

Pumpkin Topping
1 can (15 ounces)
pumpkin
1/2 cup milk
1 teaspoon cinnamon
1/2 teaspoon salt
3/4 cup sugar, divided
3 eggs, separated
1 envelope unflavored
gelatin
1/4 cup cold water

Preheat oven to 350 degrees.

Combine graham crackers, sugar and butter in a medium bowl; mix well. Press lightly in bottom of 13 x 9-inch pan.

To make filling, in a small bowl using an electric mixer, beat eggs, sugar and cream cheese. Pour over graham cracker mixture; smooth out top. Bake 20 minutes. Remove from oven and set aside to cool.

To make topping, in a saucepan mix together pumpkin, milk, cinnamon, salt, 1/2 cup of sugar and egg yolks. Cook pumpkin mixture over medium heat for 5 minutes, stirring constantly, until thick. Remove from heat.

In a small dish dissolve gelatin in water. Stir into pumpkin mixture.

In a small bowl, using electric mixer, beat egg whites until slightly stiff, add remaining 1/4 cup of sugar and beat until stiff. Fold into pumpkin mixture and pour over cream cheese mixture; smoothing to edges of pan. Chill until firm. Serve with whipped topping.

Laurel's Apple Harvest Torte

yield: 6 to 8 servings

    4 cups unpeeled diced apples
       (about 5 medium apples)
    1 cup sugar
  1/2 cup flour
    2 teaspoons baking powder
    1 egg, beaten
    1 tablespoon melted butter
    1 teaspoon vanilla
  1/2 cup chopped walnuts
  1/2 cup chopped dates
       Whipped cream, for topping

Preheat oven to 400 degrees. Grease a 9-inch square pan.

In a large bowl combine apples, sugar, flour, baking powder, egg, butter and vanilla until blended; do not overmix. Stir in nuts and dates.

Pour into prepared pan and bake 40 minutes or until apples are soft.

Cut into squares. Serve warm or cold with whipped cream.

Bread Pudding with Apple Raisin Sauce

The Apple Raisin Sauce gives this old-fashioned bread pudding a great new taste. This is a favorite recipe from my sister, Evelyn Albrecht, and is good served warm.

yield: 9 servings

10 slices whole wheat bread	***Apple Raisin Sauce***
1 egg	1¹/4 cups apple juice
3 egg whites	¹/2 cup apple butter
1¹/2 cups milk	2 tablespoons molasses
¹/4 cup sugar	¹/2 cup raisins
¹/4 cup brown sugar	¹/4 teaspoon cinnamon
1 teaspoon vanilla	¹/4 teaspoon nutmeg
¹/2 teaspoon cinnamon	¹/2 teaspoon orange zest
¹/4 teaspoon nutmeg	
¹/4 teaspoon cloves	
2 teaspoons sugar	

Preheat oven to 350 degrees. Spray an 8 x 8-inch baking pan with non-stick cooking spray. Lay slices of bread in pan in two rows overlapping like shingles.

In a medium bowl using an electric mixer, beat together egg, egg whites, milk, sugar, brown sugar and vanilla. Pour over bread. In a small bowl, stir together cinnamon, nutmeg, cloves and sugar. Sprinkle mixture over bread pudding.

Bake bread pudding 30 to 35 minutes, until brown on top and firm to the touch.

To make Apple Raisin Sauce, in a medium saucepan stir together apple juice, apple butter, molasses, raisins, cinnamon, nutmeg and orange zest. Over low heat, bring to a simmer. Let sauce simmer for 5 minutes. Serve bread pudding warm from the oven with the warmed Apple Raisin Sauce spooned over each serving.

Steamed Cherry Pudding

*In honor of Wisconsin's sesquicentennial we offer
this favorite cherry dessert, which was served at many hotels
in Ephraim and is still popular today. Enjoy...*

yield: 8 to 10 servings

2 cups pitted tart cherries	*Sauce*
2 teaspoons baking soda	1/2 pound butter (2 sticks)
1/3 cup warm water	2 cups sugar
11/2 cups flour	1 cup half-and-half
1/4 cup sugar	
1/2 teaspoon salt	
1/4 cup molasses	

Drain cherries well in a colander. Preheat oven to 350 degrees. Grease a mold or a round baking dish with butter. (I use a round stainless steel bowl.)

In a small bowl dissolve baking soda in warm water. In a large bowl, with electric mixer, combine flour, sugar, salt, molasses and water-soda mixture; blend well. Stir drained cherries into dough mixture. Spread evenly into baking dish.

Place baking dish in a 13 x 9-inch cake pan filled with one inch of hot water. Bake one hour. Remove from oven and take baking dish out of the pan of water.

Invert cherry pudding from baking dish onto a serving platter.

To make sauce, cream butter and sugar in a large bowl with an electric mixer. In a double boiler heat half-and-half just to boiling point. Slowly mix half-and-half into butter-sugar mixture until blended. Spoon warm sauce over each serving of steamed cherry pudding.

Marvelous Brownies

*My granddaughter, Britta Jacobson, makes these delicious,
rich brownies, a recipe of her great-grandmother, Laurel.
It is a special treat when served with vanilla ice cream.*

yield: 12 servings

1/2	cup butter (1 stick)
1	cup sugar
2	eggs
1	teaspoon vanilla
1/2	cup flour
1/4	teaspoon salt
2	squares (1 ounce each) unsweetened baking chocolate
1	cup chopped nuts

Preheat oven to 350 degrees. Spray an 8-inch square cake pan
with non-stick cooking spray.

In a mixing bowl using an electric mixer, cream butter and sugar.
Add eggs one at a time, beating well. Mix in vanilla. Slowly beat
flour and salt into creamed mixture.

Melt chocolate in microwave for 35 to 40 seconds. Add to
creamed mixture; stir in nuts.

Spread into prepared pan; bake 20 minutes. Do not overbake.
Brownie top should be soft when touched with fingers.

Cool in pan and cut into squares.

Peanut Butter Bars

When my granddaughter, Elaine, makes cookies this is her favorite recipe.
Her sisters love the peanut butter and chocolate taste.

yield: 15 bars

- 1 **cup peanut butter**
- 1/2 **cup light corn syrup**
- 1/2 **cup brown sugar**
- 1/2 **cup powdered sugar**
- 2 **tablespoons margarine**
- 2 **cups rolled oats**

Topping
- 1 **cup chocolate chips**
- 2 **tablespoons peanut butter**

In a medium saucepan, heat peanut butter, corn syrup, brown sugar, powdered sugar and margarine on medium to low heat, until margarine is melted. Stir frequently. Remove from heat. Stir in oats and blend well. Press into an ungreased 9-inch cake pan.

Put chocolate chips in a medium microwave-safe dish. Microwave on high 1 minute, stirring every 30 seconds until smooth. Stir in peanut butter and blend well. Spread on top of peanut butter mixture in pan.

Chill in refrigerator until chocolate topping is firm. Cut into bars to serve.

Laurel's Lemon Tart

yield: 12 to 15 servings

Crust
2 1/2 cups crushed graham crackers
     (about 12 whole crackers)
1/3 cup sugar
1/2 cup butter (1 stick), melted

Filling
1 package (3 ounces) lemon Jello
1 1/4 cups boiling water
1/3 cup honey
1/8 teaspoon salt
3 tablespoons lemon juice
1 teaspoon grated lemon zest
1 can (12 ounces) evaporated milk, well chilled

For crust, combine graham crackers, sugar and butter. Press half of the mixture into bottom of a 13 x 9-inch pan.

To make filling, in a medium bowl dissolve Jello in boiling water, add honey, salt, lemon juice and rind. Stir until well blended. Place bowl in refrigerator and let congeal slightly, about 15 minutes.

In a large bowl using an electric mixer beat milk until stiff peaks form. Pour Jello mixture into milk and beat well. Pour lemon mixture in crust. Sprinkle the remaining graham cracker mixture on top. Chill. Serve with whipped cream topping.

Lemon Pie

yield: 6 servings

1 1/2 cups water
1 1/2 cups sugar
1 tablespoon butter
1/4 cup cornstarch
1/4 cup cold water
3 egg yolks
Juice of 1 lemon (about 3 tablespoons)
1 teaspoon grated lemon zest
1 pie shell (8 inches), baked

Meringue
3 egg whites
6 tablespoons sugar

In a large saucepan, combine water, sugar and butter; cook over medium heat until sugar dissolves. Blend cornstarch with cold water and add to sugar-butter mixture. Cook until clear, about 5 minutes.

In a medium bowl, use a wire whisk to beat egg yolks. Take a small amount, about 3/4 cup, of sugar-butter mixture and stir into egg yolks. Slowly stir egg yolks into sugar-butter mixture and cook 2 minutes stirring constantly. Remove from heat and add lemon juice and zest. Cool; pour into baked pie shell.

Preheat oven to 350 degrees.

To make meringue, in a small bowl using an electric mixer, beat egg whites stiff, but not dry; gradually beat in sugar. Spread over cooled pie, sealing up to edge of crust, to keep meringue from shrinking. Bake approximately 12 minutes or until top is brown.

Key Lime Pie

Whenever my daughter, Shelley, goes to Florida, she likes to try different kinds of Key lime pie. This one is especially good and she likes to make it with Key lime juice brought back from Florida.

yield: 6 to 8 servings

Graham Cracker Crust
- 18 graham crackers, crushed or 1½ cups crumbs
- 1/3 cup sugar
- 1/2 cup butter (1 stick), melted

Filling
- 1 can (14 ounces) sweetened condensed milk
- 4 egg yolks
- 1/2 cup Key lime juice
- 1 container (12 ounces) whipped topping

Grease a 9-inch pie pan.

In a small bowl, combine graham crackers, sugar and butter; mix well. Press firmly in prepared pan. Chill 1 hour.

To make filling, combine milk and egg yolks in a medium saucepan. Over low heat cook mixture while stirring, about 10 minutes, being careful to not let mixture boil. Remove from heat to cool slightly. Beat mixture while slowly adding lime juice. Fold in whipped topping. Pour into crust and refrigerate overnight.

Door County Cherry Pie

Cherry pie is the all-time favorite pie in Door County.
My mother began baking cherry pies when my dad and grandpa Ed
both had cherry orchards. Picking cherries wasn't always fun,
but the reward of a fresh cherry pie made up for it.

yield: 8 servings

Crust	*Filling*
2 cups flour	3 cups pitted cherries,
1 teaspoon salt	fresh or frozen and
3/4 cup shortening	thawed
4 to 5 tablespoons ice water	1 cup sugar
	2 1/4 tablespoons tapioca
	1/4 teaspoon salt
	1 tablespoon butter

Preheat oven to 400 degrees.

In a large bowl combine flour and salt; cut in shortening with a pastry blender until pieces are the size of large peas. Then add ice water, a little at a time until all the flour is moistened and dough holds together. Divide pastry into two parts and form into balls. Roll out on lightly floured board to 1/8-inch thickness. Line a 9-inch pie pan with bottom crust, trim the dough to within 1/2 inch of the edge of pan.

In a large bowl combine cherries, sugar, tapioca and salt. Let stand for 15 minutes. Pour cherry mixture into pie crust; dot with butter. Cover with top crust, and cut slits for steam to escape. Pinch the edges together with thumb and index finger to seal; flute decoratively.

Bake 45 minutes to 1 hour until crust is brown.

Applesauce Spice Cake

yield: 10 to 12 servings

3/4 **cup margarine** **(11/2 sticks)**	***Caramel Frosting***
11/2 **cups sugar**	1/2 **cup butter (1 stick)**
2 **eggs**	1 **cup brown sugar**
21/2 **cups flour**	1/4 **cup milk**
11/2 **teaspoons baking soda**	2 **cups powdered sugar**
1/2 **teaspoon salt**	
1 **teaspoon cinnamon**	
1/4 **teaspoon cloves**	
1/2 **teaspoon nutmeg**	
2 **cups applesauce**	
1 **cup chopped nuts**	
1 **cup raisins**	

Preheat oven to 350 degrees. Grease and flour a 13 x 9-inch pan.

Using an electric mixer cream together margarine and sugar in a large bowl. Add eggs one at a time, beating after each addition.

In a medium bowl, stir together flour, baking soda, salt, cinnamon, cloves and nutmeg. Add flour mixture and applesauce alternately to creamed batter. Mix well. Stir in nuts and raisins. Pour into pan and bake 40 to 45 minutes.

To make frosting, in a saucepan melt butter, stir in brown sugar; bring to a boil stirring for 2 minutes. Stir in milk and return to a boil, stirring constantly. Remove from heat; cool to lukewarm. Add powdered sugar and blend with an electric mixer until smooth. Cover top of spice cake with frosting.

Chocolate Fudge Cake

*The summer Shelley learned how to make this cake,
she found it easy and a big hit, so she baked it more than once a week.
Now her daughter, Laurel, is baking it often for her parents
and brother Steve.*

yield: 15 servings

1 2/3 cups flour	***Quick Fudge Frosting***
1 1/2 cups sugar	4 cups powdered sugar
2/3 cup cocoa	6 tablespoons cocoa
1 1/2 teaspoons baking soda	1/4 teaspoon salt
1 teaspoon salt	7 tablespoons boiling
1/2 cup shortening	water
1 1/2 cups buttermilk	1/2 teaspoon vanilla
1 teaspoon vanilla	1/4 cup butter (1/2 stick),
2 eggs	softened

Preheat oven to 350 degrees. Grease and lightly flour a
13 x 9-inch baking pan.

In a large bowl using an electric mixer, blend flour, sugar, cocoa,
baking soda and salt. Mix in shortening, buttermilk and vanilla.
Add the eggs and beat 2 minutes. Pour into prepared pan. Bake
40 to 45 minutes or until wooden pick inserted into center comes
out clean. Remove pan from oven to cool.

To make frosting stir together powdered sugar, cocoa and salt in
a large bowl. Add water, vanilla and butter. Beat together until
smooth and of spreading consistency. Spread on cooled cake.

Annie's Homemade Ice Cream

One of our waitresses, Elaine Zarse, shared her grandma Annie Olson's recipe with us. When we served three meals a day at the hotel, my dad would make homemade ice cream, hand turned, for Sunday noon chicken dinner. We can still taste how good it was. You should have a bag of ice cubes and rock salt handy to put around container in ice cream freezer. My dad, Floyd, used a block of ice from the ice house and rock salt. (Follow manufacturer's instructions when using an electrically powered ice-cream maker.)

yield: 1 quart

1	cup milk
5	cups heavy cream, divided
5	egg yolks
1	cup sugar
1/8	teaspoon salt
2	teaspoons vanilla

Scald milk and 1 1/2 cups of the cream in a double boiler.

In a separate bowl beat egg yolks; add sugar and salt. Slowly stir mixture into scalded milk. Cook in double boiler 5 minutes or until mixture coats the back of a wooden spoon. Remove from heat to cool.

When cool, stir in the remaining 1 1/2 cups cream. Put into an old-fashioned hand-cranked freezer and churn until ready to serve, about 20-30 minutes.

Mrs. Norman's Fudge Sauce

This was a favorite recipe from our friend, Jeanette Norman
who helped prepare food for our smorgasbord.
We always served this fudge sauce with ice cream.
It is really good served warm. For chocolate lovers only.

yield: 15 servings

1 cup sugar
1 tablespoon flour
2 tablespoons butter
1 cup evaporated milk or 1 cup milk
2 tablespoons cocoa or 2 squares
  unsweetened chocolate, melted

Blend together sugar and flour in a small bowl.

In a double boiler, mix together butter, milk and chocolate over low heat until melted. Stir in sugar-flour mixture and cook until thickened.

Crisp Oatmeal Cookies

When my mother baked these cookies at Christmastime, she stored them
in airtight containers on our upstairs landing. My sisters and I would
grab a handful on our way to our bedrooms to eat in bed.
I wonder if she ever noticed.

yield: 5 1/2 dozen

1	**cup butter (2 sticks)**
1	**cup sugar**
1	**cup brown sugar**
2	**eggs**
1	**teaspoon vanilla**
1 1/2	**cups flour**
3	**cups rolled oats**
1	**teaspoon baking soda**
1/2	**teaspoon salt**
1/2	**cup chopped nuts**

Preheat oven to 350 degrees.

In a large bowl using an electric mixer, cream together butter,
sugar, brown sugar, eggs and vanilla. Add flour, oats, baking soda,
salt and nuts to creamed mixture and mix well.

Shape dough into 2 log-shaped rolls, approximately 15 inches
long and 2 1/2 inches in diameter. Wrap in waxed paper and chill
thoroughly. Slice logs into 1/4-inch thick pieces. Place on
ungreased baking sheet. Bake 10 minutes or until lightly browned.

Oatmeal Raisin Cookies

My sister, Grace, makes these oatmeal cookies often for her family,
and it's a favorite treat with our family as well.
Grace adds a half cup of chocolate chips to hers.

yield: 21/2 dozen

1 **cup solid vegetable shortening**
1 **cup sugar**
1 **cup brown sugar**
1 **teaspoon vanilla**
2 **eggs**
11/2 **cups flour**
3 **cups rolled oats**
1 **teaspoon baking soda**
1 **teaspoon cinnamon**
1 **cup raisins**
1/2 **cup chopped nuts**

Preheat oven to 350 degrees.

In a large bowl using an electric mixer, cream together shortening, sugar and brown sugar. Add vanilla and eggs; beat until well mixed.

In a medium bowl, stir together flour, oats, baking soda, and cinnamon. Add to creamed mixture and mix until dough is blended. Stir in raisins and nuts.

Bake 10 to 12 minutes on a lightly greased baking sheet.

Laurel's Sugar Cookies

yield: 5 dozen

11/2 **cups sugar, divided**
1 **cup butter (2 sticks)**
3 **eggs**
1 **teaspoon vanilla**
3 **cups flour**
1 **teaspoon baking soda**
1 **teaspoon salt**
1 **teaspoon cream of tartar**

Cream 1 cup of sugar and butter in a large bowl using an electric mixer until light and fluffy. Add eggs and vanilla; beat for 2 minutes.

Gradually add flour, baking soda, salt and cream of tartar into creamed mixture until well blended. Chill in refrigerator for several hours.

Preheat oven to 350 degrees. Spray two baking sheets with non-stick cooking spray.

Form dough into 11/2 inch balls and place 2 inches apart on prepared sheets. Put remaining 1/2 cup of sugar in a small bowl, grease bottom of a small glass, dip glass in sugar and press down lightly on each cookie. Repeat dipping process for each cookie.

Bake 10 minutes or until lightly browned. Remove from oven and cool on board or wire rack.

Chocolate Window Cookies

When you slice these cookies they have the look of church windows.

yield: about 4 dozen

- 1 **package (12 ounces) chocolate chips**
- 1/2 **cup margarine (1 stick)**
- 1 **egg, beaten**
- 1 **package (10 1/2 ounces) colored
mini-marshmallows**
- 1 **cup chopped walnuts**
- 1 **cup coconut**

In a saucepan melt chocolate chips and margarine over low heat. Add egg, stirring constantly for 5 minutes. Let mixture cool for 5 minutes.

Mix marshmallows and nuts in a medium bowl and pour chocolate mixture over the top and mix together.

Tear off 2 sheets of waxed paper, each about 24 inches long. Divide mixture in half on each sheet. Place mixture along the center in a long row, leaving about 3 inches at each end of the paper free of mixture. Sprinkle 1/2 cup of coconut on top of each half.

With your hands, form a log by wrapping the waxed paper around each row of mixture and roll it over until it forms a log 1 1/2 inches in diameter and about 18 inches long. Scotch tape ends to close rolls.

Chill several hours in the refrigerator before slicing. Slice each piece about 1/2 inch thick.

Spicy Moravian Cookies

Moravian cookies are a thin, crisp, and spicy specialty brought from Europe in the 18th century. It is a delicious cookie still popular today.

yield: 6 dozen

1	**cup molasses**
1/2	**cup butter (1 stick)**
1	**teaspoon baking soda**
1 3/4	**teaspoons baking powder**
2 1/4	**cups flour**
1	**teaspoon salt**
1	**teaspoon ginger**
1/2	**teaspoon cloves**
1/2	**teaspoon cinnamon**
1/2	**teaspoon nutmeg**

Heat molasses to boiling in a large saucepan. Remove from heat.

Pour molasses into a large mixing bowl and stir in butter. Add baking soda, baking powder, flour, salt, ginger, cloves, cinnamon and nutmeg; blend well.

Chill in refrigerator for 8 hours or overnight.

Preheat oven to 350 degrees.

Roll out dough 1/16-inch thick on lightly floured board or pastry cloth. Cut dough with cookie cutter in desired shapes.

Place on lightly greased baking sheet and bake 5 to 7 minutes.

Pumpkin Cookies

This is a favorite cookie from Janel Vernon,
who says they are a must for Halloween.

yield: 3 dozen

1/2	cup butter (1 stick)
11/2	cups sugar
1	egg
1	cup canned pumpkin
1	teaspoon vanilla
21/2	cups flour
1	teaspoon baking powder
1	teaspoon baking soda
1/2	teaspoon salt
1	teaspoon nutmeg
1	teaspoon cinnamon
1	cup chocolate chips

Preheat oven to 350 degrees. Spray 2 baking sheets with non-stick cooking spray.

In a large bowl using an electric mixer, cream butter and sugar until fluffy. Beat in egg, pumpkin and vanilla.

In a separate bowl, stir together flour, baking powder, baking soda, salt, nutmeg and cinnamon; add to creamed mixture and blend. Stir in chocolate chips. Drop by rounded tablespoon about 2 inches apart on prepared sheets and bake 15 minutes.

Fruit Pizza

*My daughter, Shelley, entered this dessert recipe in our local
Scandinavian festival bake-off, and won second place.
The fresh fruit makes it "eye catching" and it tastes good.*

yield: 16 small servings

1 **package sugar cookie refrigerator dough**
1 **package (8 ounces) cream cheese**
1 **tablespoon milk**
1 **teaspoon grated orange zest**
1 **peach, sliced**
1 **cup sliced strawberries**
1 **cup blueberries**
1 **kiwi, sliced**

Preheat oven to 350 degrees.

Press sugar cookie dough into a 12-inch round pizza pan. Bake
7 to 9 minutes or until edges are light brown. Cool completely.

In a small mixing bowl beat together cream cheese, milk and
orange zest. Spread mixture over the baked cookie dough. Cover
the entire top with fruit, arranging fruit into concentric circles;
peaches, strawberries, blueberries, kiwi or any combination of
fresh fruit.

Slice in wedges to serve.

Index

INDEX